Elemental Birth Imprints:

*Living and Evolving
with the Earth's Elementals, NOW!*

Activating your Pre-Personality Self

Marilyn & Tohmas Twintreess

This BOOK comes to you with all our blessings and love!

Ahhh~Muse
2340 Highway 180 East #171
Silver City, New Mexico 88061 USA
www.AhhhMuse.com • MQT@AhhhMuse.com
575-534-0410 • 575-654-4757
We so love hearing from you~

Copyright©2012 Marilyn & Tohmas Twintreess
All Rights Reserved. No part of this book may be reproduced in any form or by any means, electronic or mechanical, including photocopying, recording, or by any information storage and retrieval system, without permission in writing from the publishers, except for brief quotations embodied in literary articles or reviews.

First Edition
Printed in the United States of America
ISBN# 978-1-890808-14-3
Cover Photo by: Leonardo Martins, Rio de Janeiro, Brazil
Graphic Design: Charlotte Krebs of Salmagundi Design

Welcome~
Thank you for so kindly respecting our copyright of this material.
This information came to us in such sacred ways,
it is our job to honor it exactly as it came to us.
We trust that you understand and appreciate that; that's why you're here!

Enjoy abundantly!

Dedication!

*As you are about to feel right down to your toes,
we love dedicating these pages of our lives—
which magically turn into BOOKS—
to You,
reading this and opening your heart to who knows what, you brave soul!*

*We dedicate this to our Spiritfamilies,
the Muses in our constant Creativity
that make Life! possible and magnificent always.
We dedicate this to the Elementals and the Earth Mother
for inviting humans to quantum-leap-evolve in this beautiful breath now
and having the grace and compassion to hold space while we are taking the TIME to do so, NOW!*

*Now is the Time.
Now is the Time for Wow!*

Welcome to Elemental Birth Imprints

Dive in!

We already have.

Though we don't understand the fullness of these Imprints, we are living them.

With all our bodies, hearts and Spirit interwoven we invite you: LIVE Elemental Birth Imprints along side of us.

Let's co-create our future in the present while honoring the past that is eternally guiding and accepting us.

Testimonials

~living this wisdom daily I feel more alive and at peace with who I am!
~more profound and real than I could have imagined and more practical and applicable than I would have believed.
~knowing my Imprint has taught me a language that my soul had known in feeling and now my mind does too!
~ Thank You Tohmas and Marilyn for continuing to listen to Spirit and be guided with your hearts!
So much LOVE!!!

—**Jen** *(Earth/Fire 55%/45%)*

Knowing my Conception and Birth Elemental Imprints has supported me in examining my energies at any given moment; which has empowered me to calm the waters and cool the fires within my beingness so that everyone around me responds in a positive way in that moment of timelessness. I am forever grateful for this gift of the Elemental Imprints, they have changed my life and those around me. Namaste`

— **Mary Nelson, founder of LaStone Therapy** *(Fire/Water 55%/45%)*

Elemental Birth Imprints are such a wonderful way to get to know your true self!
After Learning about our EBI's, we are more able to accept and to love our nature and our being,
enabling us to "bring along our shadow parts" as we live each day fully.
EBIs also support us in relating with each other and to our students and employees who also know their EBIs, and we have so much fun discussing about all of it! It has brought all of us closer into relationships that honor each other.

—**Hiro and Hana, Happy Happy Crystal School, Tokyo, Japan** *(Hiro: Ethers/Earth 90%/10% & Hana: Earth/Fire 60%/40%)*

"Hi! I am Air-Earth, actually, 80% Air and 20% Earth . . . and you are? . . . Happy to meet and know you! I am happy to meet and know myself!

Indeed, when Grandmother Sweet Shield and the Twintrees offered my Elemental Birth Imprint, I resonated, and continue to resonate to this day, with the core of my being. By knowing my core elemental response to life, by knowing my most basic simple components, I feel I access me! And along this path of knowing myself more and more, all of Nature supports my journey: all of life's ever changing and moving Elementals show, teach, and mirror to me. It is all so accessible! And for everyone too!

When I first received my EBI, I felt I "got it", I understood why I love Earth so much and seek to be with Nature so much. And with the Twintrees additional wisdom offered to me: " be ok with your Air, accept your Air", I observed myself and faced all those trillion ideas of mine, all those projects that I wish to accomplish, all the changes that I live and trigger, all the freedom ideals and all the attachments; no longer were they issues, I, then and there, chose to perceive and utilize them as part of my strength. How relieving and empowering!

And then, when I learned of my family members' EBI, I understood their ways of contributing to my own evolution. Both my daughters' EBI are composed of Fire and Water; the exact compliments to my Air-Earth! Well, how perfect a match-up is that! Regularly, my dear Fire-Water daughter will burst out intense emotion and when it has all been expressed and passed, she'll come back to me and say "sorry about all that mom... it was my fire, it could be intense sometimes . . .' !
Thank you Grandmother and Twintrees for offering this wisdom to us all: simple, basic & profound!"

—**Mitsi, Ottawa, Canada** *(Air/Earth 80%/20%)*

~ offers a foundation for communication...so we human beings can better understand each other . . .

—**Kelly** *(Ethers/Fire 80%/20%)*

Thank You Tohmas and Marilyn Twintrees!
Since I have met you both, your integrity and commitment to the Earth and all Her creations has been inspiring and consistent. And now that I have experienced the Elemental Birth Imprint workshops, I have an even deeper respect and understanding of the gift that you offer us all.

Since understanding our world and our relationships is such a core desire deep in all of us, understanding the balance and dance of the Elementals is such a tremendously important part of this. When you think about it, what is a deeper core than our Elemental makeup?

Understanding how my own Elemental Imprint interacts with others is the most profound learning that I have taken from your work. There is at least one situation each day that presents itself that is easier to read and deal with smoothly and with grace by applying information gained in the Elemental Birth Imprint Workshops. Please let me know when you are planning to be in town again for the next one! Many Blessings!

—**David** *(Water/Fire 85%/15%)*

Practice is always perfect.

Each day of life, we listen to our Spirit families. We talk together a lot like we would with other friends. We take our questions, our lessons and our deepest feelings to our Spirits. They generously answer us back in words. They show us, tell us how we are traveling because how we are moving looks different from the bigger- biggest- picture (thank goodness!) (literally!).

It is our Spirit family's loving mission to respond to whatever we ask and to honor us even beyond what we know how to ask; their responses always meet us at the true level where we are learning, integrating and healing (NOT WHERE WE THINK WE ARE).

This expansive bright SpiritYou always frees us to look at our healing brand new. The immensity of this ever-growing gift cannot be fully stated in words. By comparison, our defenses and unresolved traumas always look at us with unchanging eyes. For them, we never change. We never grow up. We never heal. Therefore, we must always be protected. Our hearts remain closed when we are always guarded.

Listening to Spirit enlightens us patiently one piece at a time. With them we are living, breathing, perfect, divine order. To honor this gift, our Spirits ask us to give what only we can offer in return: Our practice. When we, Marilyn and Tohmas, listen to the wisdom of our Spirit families we must act upon it. Each day, we practice their guidance with all that we are. This isn't to say that we don't fall down on the job -sometimes, we do. And we look pretty funny when it happens, rolling on the ground, looking utterly dazed. But that doesn't matter much. What matters most of all is that we get up after we fall, we clean ourselves up, we do our VERY best to laugh at our own confusion and learnings. Now. Every time. Constantly. Forever.

"We are the commitment that forms our path."

We practice what we have learned from our Spirit families, even before we understand. Of course, ultimately, this is the only way we will be able to understand. Understanding always comes after the experience. Acting upon our Spirits keeps the conversation going between us day after day. It keeps growing. Then it is utterly exponential. Who knows where we will land? Who knows what new magic we will birth? Just by offering what is possible, what is possible only for us to give, we seed the gifts of Spirit into our lives and into our world. Watch for it!

Therefore, with our finest truth we must honor you in the same way. We invite you as you listen to the wisdom of our Spirits in this Book to practice it. Yes, yes, we feel your protests, "I don't know how! I'm not good enough yet. What if I get it wrong?"

We might be hearing your voices even more than you because we've heard them inside of us so many times. Each time we have done something new those protests jump up and shout right away. Of course. It's their duty to protect us. Yet, if we kept ALWAYS listening to and acting upon our defenses we might be "safe" (probably not) . . . but who wants to be "safe" from full-out lifeforce, consciousness, love.

Practice whatever you can from this Book, from your own Spirit families, just a little bit each day. Find one thing that you can seed into this reality. The garden you are growing honors us all. Thank you.

Aligning with the Elementals

For many years our Spirit Grandmother talked with us about the Elementals. These are the Devic Spirits of the five Elements that create all form upon the Earth Mother: Earth, Fire, Water, Air and Ethers. As you read their names, jump up! Introduce yourself. Ask them what gifts they have for you right now.

All of us are made up of some perfect intricate combination of the Elementals. Everything we experience is some union of the Elementals, including thoughts, feelings, and all the children of the Earth: Animals, Plants and Minerals. That is why Grandmother speaks of the Elementals constantly. *"When you align with the Elementals you are joining with the core of life on the Earth, including the Earth Mother. It doesn't matter if you ever understand this or not. Your bodies are already speaking their language in every breath. You join subconsciously with their great creativity constantly balancing everything in your life. When you do this subconsciously you will be surprised by what happens. Life seems to take you by storm. When you are marching up the mountain it feels like you get knocked down and out constantly. Align with the Elementals* **consciously**; *then you are living and being the most natural, continually dancing flow of life. Surrender within their wisdom and spontaneity. As you do this, you will evolve. It doesn't matter how you have reached this growth, only that you do and be it. From there, everything that you are is utterly accepted. Mistakes are part of the healing, an honored part of the journey. The Elementals offer themselves as your most immediate ally in evolution and unconditional love and support."*

With words like that who wouldn't join in? We learned about the qualities of the Elementals happily each day. And before we really knew how to work with those energies, Grandmother shamelessly offered us what she called, Aligning with the Elementals. She showed us how to breathe with each one so that our bodies would both consciously and spontaneously join with their forces of life. Join us.

We are going to do and be it right now.

Aligning with the Elementals Meditation

Give yourself as much stillness and space as possible.

Unplug.

Now plug into the full vibrations of this living, breathing meditation.

Let your joining with it be uninterrupted.

When you find unrelated busy thoughts visiting you during this, let them just pass by. When you do that, they become your subconscious voices, not your conscious ones. Let them talk themselves out without you giving them extra fuel. Just love and accept them as the little unhealed parts of you that are trying to distract you from full union and evolution—your own perfect unique genius. They are only doing it because they are afraid of the unknown. You can understand that. Just love and accept every single part of you and every single voice. That will bring all of you together in conscious unlimited healing, support and profound newness that cannot be predicted.

Sit or lay comfortably during this Aligning. Keep your back as straight as possible (but not stiff) so that all breath can freely travel all parts of your body. Breath is the most immediate bridge between body and Spirit. Breathe deeply and easily in this mediation; let go of forcing your breath. Its spontaneous rhythms will absorb old pain and let it go. Allow it all. And laugh and cry and enjoy.

*We begin with the **Earth** Elemental. We align with it by breathing in and out through the nose. The entire time that we align with **Earth** just breathe in and out through the nose. Feel the full length and width and depth of your body. Be utterly aware of your form. Feel its weight sinking into the **Earth**, giving away worry and struggle. The Earth Mother receives it and transforms it. Just let go. Now all of your senses awaken. See the colors all around you. Watch how light and shadow draw shapes and geometries in everything. If you watch closely there are faces all around in trees, puppies and flowers. Hear the sounds and the silence of life filling you and emptying you. Filling and emptying. Listen so brightly, so lovingly, that you can hear your heartbeat . . . or at least hear the willingness of your beautiful body to hear that and everything. Taste and smell the air as you inhale and exhale. If any of this is uncomfortable, know that your upcoming exhales will expel your judgments and struggles. Breathe in and out through the nose uniting with the innate ease of the **Earth** Elemental. Anything that has been too difficult is transforming now. It is softening. It is moving through your reality leaving only wisdom. Smell and taste gratitude as you breathe. Touch your body as you go more deeply into your breath. Softly delight in your form. Feel how your hands revel in knowing the strength of your skin and muscles and nerves. Focus on this. Even in this quiet stillness feel the readiness of your body to act upon your finest truth. Now breathe all your senses with such gratitude that they join with your Spirit bringing you new awarenesses in each breath. This is why you are here. This is why you are upon the Earth Mother. This is one of the many gifts of the **Earth** Elemental.*

*Now we align with the **Fire** Elemental by breathing in through the mouth and out through the nose. Now we are inviting immeasurable lifeforce and creativity. Feel it warm your body and your heart. Pure life courses through your blood, your breath, your feelings. Light up every cell with its bright golden* *glow. Radiate this. When you are full of your own **Fire**, spill out over your edges. Be a gigantic huge flame—utterly alive and ready to meet every passion and inspiration. Breathe in through the mouth and out through the nose. Lifeforce is constantly changing you. This is always so you can truly feel this Now. Your bones stretch. Stiffness melts away. Unknown adventure offers itself. Your instincts awaken. As you find yourself more primal, judge nothing. Breathe. Choose to change constantly. This keeps you in the path of lifeforce and fuels you beyond your wildness whims. Act only upon the respectful intents that come to you now. Watch your flames dance higher and brighter. You are a breath of continual transformation. You cannot know who and what you will be next. Simply choose to honor it and thank the **Fire** Elemental.*

*Now we align with the **Water** Elemental breathing in through the nose and out through the mouth. We are breathing and being our own hearts. Even as you read these vibrationwords, let go, let go so fully that you do not have to understand this energy a word at a time. Let it wash over you. Its gentle and wild flow will merge with you. Together we will feel everything. Name nothing. Choose to feel and, simultaneously, to be acceptance. When pain arises to be freed, birth it with full rhythmic breaths like a mother in labor. Know that new life is coming. Always. Trust in it. Give unparalleled compassion to you and the new healings that are growing within and outside of you. When joy arises, smile. Breathe acceptance. Let it enter your heart through all of your senses. See it. Smell it. Touch it. Taste it. Hear it. Yet do not define it. Let it freely move you through every experience in life. There is hidden joy in ALL emotions when you align with the **Water** Elemental completely. Breathe in through the nose and out through the mouth. Feelings come and go without pause. You are not your feelings. You are bigger than that. You are essence choosing to feel and then to heal and then to act upon your divinity. Love and thanks to the **Water** Elemental.*

*Now we align with the **Air** Elemental breathing in and out through the mouth. Now feast upon words, thoughts, ideas and child-like curiosity. Be boldly in what you can imagine. Learn from everything. Let nothing escape your awareness. Grow your understanding from this. You are freedom. At the core of everything you are freedom. Maybe you don't believe this. Maybe you don't understand this. Breathe so richly that the next breath always brings you more opportunities to freely grow. **Air**/breath is the fastest bridge between body and Spirit. In truth, they are not really separate, yet every human feels separate regardless. In being born you separate from your mother, you grow your own body and you do not remember that it is continually connected to Spirit. Breathe now the most amazing possibilities. Breathe that the dreams that you dare to dream are you yet do not limit you. Breathe that you are already body and Spirit perfectly intertwined, ever free to think and create a new reality. Soar above the smallness of unneeded repetition. With each inhale, breathe your entire body and Spirit as free. With each exhale, breathe your entire body and Spirit as one, letting go of distrust and pain. When you dare to breathe bigger than life your dreams will match that and more. We honor freedom and **Air**.*

*Now we align with the **Ethers** Elemental. Breathe in and out through the nose. It's true. Earth, Fire, Water and Air merge seamlessly. **Ethers** is the Spirit that moves through their expressions and forms. Here we are living at our center stillness. We no longer have to try to be undistracted. We are the peace that birthed these bodies originally. It echoes in every cell. We are home. We are here. We are now. Aligning with the **Ethers** is natural. It happens without our conscious effort yet now we are joining with that consciously. We remember that Spirit embodies through us. Even when we are trying hard to be something other than what we are, our Spirits embody through us. We revel in our spontaneity and our easy conversations. They join wisdom to our willingness and we bring bigger gifts than we can understand to every moment and to every friend. We breathe in and out through the nose feeling even in our loneliness we are not alone. In all directions, in all ways, our Spirit Guides surround us. Some of their faces surprise us. Some of them are oh so familiar. We welcome them. Long have they protected and honored us far past our abilities to do these things for ourselves. It is simple now to see how every time we have fallen down our*

*Spirits have always been there waiting for us to ask for their help. In each breath now ask for the support, the love, the union, of our Spirits. Receive it as only you can. Let the **Ethers** come into you with every breath and inspire you beyond all reason. Thank you to all of the Elementals. We align with you now and every day (even when we seem to forget).*

Now you are aligning with the Elementals. Because of our fantastic experience we heartily invite you to align with the Elementals every single day (We have a CD of this aligning that is beautiful and at the ready for you also.). The more that you practice aligning with the Elementals, the more you are joined with life at the core. Feel that. You are fueling through this everything wonderful and true in your life.

Simultaneously, anything negative and unsupportive will drop away. When you align with the Elementals regularly that release happens as easily as a soft rain cleaning the trees, the flowers, and the world.

One of the most glorious parts of regularly practicing this alignment is that you will make it your own. You are forging a totally unique magnificent relationship between you and the Elementals. With that in place there is nothing you cannot do together. The Elementals make up all form and matter upon the Earth Mother. United with them in utter respect you can manifest the life and reality of your true-self-dreams. What are you waiting for?

Ask yourself, "What in my life do I want to lovingly and immediately transform with the Elementals?"

Take that answer and that unconditional intent and every day align with the Elementals. See you there . . .

Evolve Now?

Our Spiritual Grandmother has shared with us that when we align with the Elementals we are freely choosing to connect with the core of lifeforce—even when we don't immediately understand what that means—and we move and breathe with the natural flow of the Earth and all things. The Elementals constantly move like the winds of change. Sometimes the Fire Elemental is very strong burning away unneeded anger and violence. Sometimes the Water Elemental is the most potent washing away our worries leaving us clean and new to the world. All the Elementals make sure that the movement of life ever grows, ever loves, and ever balances itself out.

For humans, the Elementals help them release their most stubborn resistance. For instance, in every astrological Age upon the Earth humans absorb and learn the lessons of the qualities of that Age. For example, during the Piscean Age humans heal their addictions, denials, co-dependency and martyrdom, they take on the splendor of union, empathy, perfection and inspiration. Then, at the end of each Age, the Elementals have helped humans release the hardest of those struggles and learnings through elemental forces like flood, ice, storm and earthquakes (Got your attention now, didn't we?). It is their gift. They move unresolved human emotions. They unstick what is stuck. That graciously allows humans to go to the next Age and learn new tools and new healing while simultaneously integrating the old lessons as best they can.

For the first time in the story of humankind, the Earth Mother is inviting people to evolve **completely** with her. Translation: we do not <u>require</u> elemental "disasters" just to grow to the next level of consciousness. Instead, like the Earth Mother, the Elementals are generously inviting us to work *with* them; they are welcoming us to align with them so that we can heal ourselves fully, all at once.

Are you still breathing?

Hint: now would be a superb time to breathe with the Elementals.

Any one of us has the complete freedom, power and will to choose our own full-out evolution. The exponentially expanding energy upon the Earth kindly makes this possible. There are so many potentials, energy, and transformation pulsating all around us and within us that we are receiving a magnanimous boost to our innate desire to be free and enlightened. As we choose to consciously align with the Elementals, we can open up every cell of our beings to receive unlimited lifeforce and almost unbelievable change. If we willingly absorb this we will heal. We will accept all our experiences, lifetimes/parallels, especially all previously unloved emotions. We will clear ourselves of unneeded struggle, pain and separation.

You feel this. You *know* this. Your body twitches. Every day you say, "Everything is getting so much faster and faster, I can hardly keep up anymore." Good! The acceleration deeply encourages you to just leave behind baggage that never served you in the first place. Luckily you are moving too fast to miss it. The Elementals not only support us freeing ourselves from old cycles of pain and struggle, they embolden us. When we align with them we enter the new Age clearly and seamlessly flowing with all the natural rhythms of the Earth and life. The Elementals help us integrate this newness. Then our repeating cycles come from our true destinies: We are loving co-creators with the Earth Mother and our Spirits.

It is happening . . .

As you read these words your body absorbs them. As much as you allow, your heart opens within them and you align with the Elementals and all the things that are happy for your true growth, healing and love. Perhaps you were not completely aware that each word here has been birthed from full prana and unconditional acceptance. So we are saying it out loud now. Feel your every cell lighting up. Instead of only reading, all your senses are awakening and expanding with the joyous vibrations in this book/gift.

Join us. It wouldn't hurt if you were smiling really big right now! Let's *consciously* ritualize this whole body/soul experience by being here now:

*We are aligning with the **Earth** Elemental. We do this by breathing in and out through the nose. Sit up straight so that your chakra column is free, moving and growing. You do not have to close your eyes in order to align with Elementals. We are fully awake and present. In every breath we invite ourselves to align with the **Earth** Elemental <u>while</u> we are walking, talking, working, playing and smiling. Aligning with the Elementals is a gift to be carried with us in every act. So as you breathe and read and awaken, feel the full depth of your body. Breathe over every bone, muscle and nerve. See how your pranic breath automatically releases old struggle and strengthens your stamina and intent. You are fully Alive! Listen to your body. It shows you this splendiferously! It will also show you where you are not yet conscious. Rejoice in this. And give those parts of your body **Earth** Elemental breath now.*

Separation, Union and EBI's

In every moment, in every event, the Elementals dance in some perfect combination of Earth, Fire, Water, Air, Ethers. For every one here now, a peak of Elemental activity imprints us and that happens just before we are born.

Humans have a very special destiny on the Earth. They are the only beings who experience "separation" from their Spirits and from the other life forms on the Earth Mother. Everything else here, at the core, is in union. Humans experience a seeming separation from *everything* once they leave their mother's womb and take their first breath. Yet, while they are in utero, they are naturally still in union with the flows of life and still easily connect to their Spirits. The Elementals intentionally mark this last moment of union for each of us by giving us an Elemental Birth Imprint.

We carry this Imprint within us so that when we awaken to our fullness (which means that we consciously recognize that we are <u>still</u> in union with all things regardless of the seeming results of our experiences), we unite: separation/unity, dark/light, ignorance/wisdom—all polarities come together as a single unconditional gift of love. We are here on the Planet to consciously offer our well-earned union and then co-creatorship, to all of Life. Yes!

All of us awaken and heal in absolute perfect ways and timing. For us, Marilyn and Tohmas, our journey offered us Elemental Birth Imprints. Discovering them completely reminds us that we are inevitably and utterly linked to all life here. We consciously realize that we are our Spirits embodied, always have been, always will be. Upon learning our Imprints, we spontaneously recognized that our souls gave us this Imprint so that we could come back home to ourselves . . . immediately . . . constantly . . . always. Our Elemental Birth Imprints gently and insistently guide us in everything and every moment. It fills us with great joy and purpose sharing this gift with you. We have experienced that it is the <u>most core</u> reminder of our divinity that we can offer any human. It is simple. It is direct. It is our evolution now.

The Imprint...

Every human is given the gift of an Elemental Birth Imprint, the last moment before being born. Only humans receive this because on this Earth, only humans experience and practice separation from their Spirit and the natural flows of life here.

Most humans receive the energy of simply 2 Elementals imprinting them (e.g. Earth and Fire.) However, it is possible to have any number of the five Elementals in your Imprint, including also the potential to have a double Elemental Imprint (e.g. Air and Air). The order of your Elemental Birth Imprint tells you which Elemental most influences you. For example, if you are a Fire/Water Imprint then the Fire Elemental is the strongest Elemental you are choosing to work with in this lifetime. Water is the second most important Elemental for you then. When we offer E.B.I.'s we also offer them in percentages. So that Fire/Water we used as an example could be 70/30 or 60/40, etc.

The first (highest percentage) Elemental in your E.B.I. is your totem guide. You and your soul have chosen to learn about and heal with this Elemental primarily. The second Elemental (or the lower percentage, or however many follow after the first one) is your m.o. It shows how you express the qualities of the first Elemental. For example, if you are an Air/Water, you are learning about thinking, communication and learning. You will mostly *express* that through your relationship with Water (emotions). Later on we will go over how different E.B.I.'s tend to think, feel and act. For now, we will simply keep on defining the parameters of an E.B.I. so that you can integrate that well enough to act upon it in any situation.

There are two more basic qualities to an E.B.I. One is the percentage of the Elementals. In our experience, many people tend to have E.B.I.'s that are in the percentage range of 70/30 to 80/20. This seems to offer enough difference between the Elementals so that people can learn readily and clearly within our paradigms of polarity and separation.

If your percentages are higher than 80/20, likely you are focusing your learnings in very specialized areas. Your soul encourages you to repeat different levels of the same thing. On the positive side, you will manifest a great deal. You will evolve. You will grow your chosen wisdom. The shadow side can be obsession, stubbornness and a lack of objectivity.

When your percentages are less than 70/30, you tend to cooperate more between the different parts of self and your environment. On the positive side, you are versatile, continually learning new things and able to balance things with others. The negative expression of this is that you can delude yourself that you are balanced just as you are without any effort or growth. Remember, whatever your percentages are, they are absolutely PERFECT for you. This is not about trying to change them (or your E.B.I.) to some ideal number. They are already matched to your needs for learning and healing. Just accept them completely. Then you are utterly free to express them in your completely unique and continually evolving way.

One more thing about percentages: Most people receive them in increments of tens like you have seen above— 70/30 or 80/20 or fives, like 55/45 or 65/35. Yet, every once in a while some unique person will be given an 88/12 or 51/49. We feel the innate power of those numbers, yet we don't know exactly what they mean. We simply feel sure that those exact numbers bring very precise influences to those people. If you are one of these people, please listen to your numbers and feel their vibration. Be patient enough to let them speak in the numerological and geometric ways. This will inform YOU perfectly, just as it is meant to be.

The other quality of E.B.I.'s is whether or not they are symbiotic or non-symbiotic. Symbiotic Imprints are: **Earth/Water**, **Water/Earth**, **Fire/Air**, and **Air/Fire**. These combinations of Elementals innately and easily fuel each other. Can you see that? **Earth** gives structure and form to **Water** which the **Water** would not have by itself. Simultaneously, **Water** is absorbed by **Earth**, continually and simply: It fuels the Earth to easily grow minerals and gardens. Or in the case of **Air** and **Fire**, **Air** expands the natural expression of **Fire**—it directs it spontaneously. **Fire** easily heats up **Air** creating warmth and weather.

If you have a symbiotic E.B.I. you often manifest quickly and easily. You establish set routines and you frequently understand yourself and the world around you well. When you are balanced, you can make anything wonderful happen. You flow with all of life inherently. The shadow side of a symbiotic Imprint is getting mired in its own opinions. These people can be so stubborn that they never change and forever believe they are right no matter what.

A non- symbiotic E.B.I. means those Elementals still combine; however, sometimes it takes extra energy and effort to happen gracefully. If you are in balance acting upon a non-synergistic E.B.I., challenges do not deter you. You innately feel life is about learning. You are comfortable learning in order to do whatever you truly choose. Often, you have spent valuable time finding out what your greatest priorities truly are.

The shadow side of a non- symbiotic Imprint can be a fragmented person—someone who does not easily recognize all their different qualities and parts. Sometimes their defenses hide from them exactly what they need to heal to be whole and free. These people can find it difficult to understand themselves and others.

Qualities of the Elementals

Through time and space, humans have experienced the world. Or have they? Maybe that's just our way of <u>defining</u> things so that we are safe or so that we can agree to agree about what we know and understand.

Let's just throw that out the window. Now we are pure lifeforce—instincts at the ready—breath greeting life at the core every second (it is *fun* and scary, too). Now what do you know? Stop. Breathe more deeply. Actually reach out your breath like free, dancing antennae. What, and how, are you living?

Now you are breathing territory that we love: You are diving into the core of life itself and meeting us there. Your body is vibrating. *How do you know the world now?* For us, at the most core places, it is made up of the five Elements. Everything upon the Earth, including Her, is comprised of these Elements or combinations of them. Again, because we have walked and talked with the Elements (**Earth, Fire, Air, Water, Ethers**) we have learned, loved and co-created with the **Elementals**—the Spirits/Totems/Consciousness of the Elements.

Yes, yes, we have *talked* about them already. Yet, in this part of this BOOK we are talking about the qualities of the Elementals. Of course, you can't really just talk about them. They beg to be **experienced**. The Elementals live and breathe very close to your instincts . . . your beating heart . . . your flashes of inspiration, hunger or passion. Call all of your senses to alert! We will give you words about each of the qualities of the Elementals. What you can't see—but you will FEEL as you wish—is that each and every one of those words gifts itself to you from our real world experience of and with the Elementals.

Just to impart this, we had to align with the Elementals first . . . just as you have already done in other parts of this living BOOK (by the way, feel free—VERY FREE—to pause these words and align with the Elementals. Jump with them, dance with them, eat live, raw food with them. Anytime. You don't need our permission.).

To truly know the qualities of the Elementals you have to JUMP in with all your fingers and toes and wide-awake senses and willingness: You must become each of the Elements, one at a time as we talk about them. Our words are just happy guides. If and when your perfect and personal experience takes you down other paths or shades of meaning from the Elementals, go! Do not walk. Run, skip and leap!

We always introduce the Elementals in the same order: **Earth**, **Fire**, **Water**, **Air** and **Ethers**. We begin with the **Earth**. Here is where you meet your body. Every human with their own perfect soul has chosen from the most love possible to be here now. That choice is awakened and experienced with the **Earth** Elemental. Remember, all of the qualities of each and every Elemental are simply free energies: no judgment, no agenda, besides supporting love, acceptance and lifeforce. Humans interpret those gifts generally either positively or negatively. In every moment that is the free will choice that is left at the doorway to your heart. In each breath you will choose to positively or negatively express the Elementals.

Nowhere is this more noted and/or measured than with the **Earth** Elemental. It is here our Spirits choose to embody and co-create more life. With our bodies come five physical senses that our mainstream culture deems as proof of reality. Here we meet the bottom line as human beings.

In positively experiencing the **Earth** Elemental, we tend to meet and greet: stamina, common sense, longevity, innate wisdom, interconnectedness with life, loyalty, manifesting, prosperity and all our bodies' needs and desires. Here we meet the Earth Mother herself. If we are happy in our own skin, then likely we will honor Her. We will treat Her children kindly. We will utilize Her resources—Her gifts—with gratitude. Fully aligned with the **Earth** Elemental we dare to prosper and we work hard to make it so.

If we choose to negatively align with the **Earth** Elemental (or if we are in denial of it) we struggle being in our own bodies. Sometimes our senses are not acute. We feel challenged being a part of the seasons and the natural flows of life. Often times we think of ourselves as "battling" the Elements (just to survive). Being in survival mode only can bring on: confusion, scatteredness, continual disorientation, lack of perseverance and inability to honor others. In short, we feel the world is against us.

Practices to Support you Aligning Positively with the Earth Elemental

1. Slow down.

2. Consider before acting. That is the respect you offer all life.

3. Touch the Earth. Go barefoot. Get outside and stay there until you have come home.

4. Make friends with all your neighbors, human and non-human.

5. Move. Jump up and down! Feel your muscles, nerves, and heart work in perfect harmony.

6. Eat and drink consciously. When you fuel yourself with honorable intent, your body changes instantly. Build upon that and build a new life.

7. Be responsible to everything you do. No hints here, just do it.

8. Get up and go to sleep with the Sun. Live fully in the rhythms of the Earth.

9. Use every single resource of the Earth wisely, carefully and happily. The three R's do work: Reduce, Reuse, Recycle. We like to add a fourth R: Respect.

10. Gratitude. Begin every day finding every single thing for which you are grateful. At the end of the day, find even more things and different things to thank for their gifts. In between, take every opportunity to say thank you. Even if something has been painful, it has a special gift for you. Nothing opens the door faster to winning that gift than a heart-felt, "Thank you!" Every **Earth** experience has something precious for you . . .

11. Give complete attention and full presence to everything you do. Instead of multi-tasking, single—task it. It is pure joy to wake up, jump out of bed and squeeze every bit of your particular lifeforce and love into every single act. You could argue that most people won't notice. We are not going to argue with you. Our culture has produced a lot of sleepwalking individuals. But do you know what is really cool? YOU will know that all your acts are full to overflowing with riches and abundance. All you need to live like this is for YOU to know that truth. Everybody else will find out in their own sweet perfect time.

At the end of experiencing the qualities of each of the Elementals (and we are at the end of the **Earth** Elemental) stop. Lean into it. Become it. When you are happily satiated record summaries of your experience. It is a truism that people who feel really successful at life (in our book that means positively aligning and experiencing the Elementals), full—on live the Elementals, and then afterwards, they write about it. Or they talk about it.

Or they sing about it. That combination of living fully and recording it affirms your choices to live positively with the Elementals and your perfect lifeforce. And it just keeps on growing it . . . even on a hard day.

Now, welcome to the **Fire** Elemental. Are you breathing? We know, you think we are kidding but we are not. When you ground with the **Earth** Elemental, bring that even balancing breath to the **Fire** which is BIG and BRIGHT and JOYOUS. Just to make sure that you have buddied up with **Fire**, jump up and down! Dance! Smile at your every organ, nerve, hair and cell. When you positively integrate the warmth of **Fire**, here are some of the gifts that will quickly find you: speed; transformation; absolutely unlimited lifeforce; instincts; passion; creativity; the biggest pictures you can find; mentorship; ever bigger pictures; and just for the fun of it, chili peppers; sunrise and dayglo orange; and did we say CHANGE? When we met the **Earth** Elemental we presented ourselves with the opportunity to be full-square in our bodies, calmly present for any and all experience. Now we build upon that with the **Fire** Elemental. Once we are in the body, we can fill it beyond belief with lifeforce, infinite creativity and constant evolution . . . why not!

When you negatively align with **Fire**, here are some of the qualities you will be asked to heal: Apathy; coldness; joylessness; no initiative; no passion or inspiration; inability to support visions/dreams/others; inability to lead even when needed; denial about priorities; inability to recognize that it is all life and death.

Ways to Wake up the Positive Fire.
NOW!

1. Change.

2. Change again.

3. Change, even when you don't have to do it. Change is the only constant in life. Best to buddy up with it now.

4. Get up happy.

5. Go to bed happy.

6. Consciously choose to see the most positive, beautiful, glowing side of everything. Focus on that.

7. Tell the truth. (Not just to others, TELL YOURSELF.) Act on it relentlessly. The most positive reframers of life start from the most important place: the truth. When you are positive about life, you honor the truth.

8. Do it faster. See what happens.

9. Act upon your gut. If you are not practiced with this, get some practice.

10. Share your dreams and wonder with others. They probably hear all of your gripes. Now see if you can give them more awe than complaints.

11. Always plan for the best to happen and no matter what it is, turn it into the best thing possible.

Welcome to the Water Elemental!

Here we combine with feelings. Of all the Elementals, this one is the least defined by words. That is not a limit. That is a new and special opportunity when you are reading a BOOK (Is that what you are doing?).

More than ever open your heart. We guarantee there will be moments in aligning with the Elementals that your heart will snap shut faster than an oyster under duress. And, you probably won't even notice it—at least not right away. So notice it. Swear to yourself that in this safe oasis, here, you will keep opening and opening your heart. And immediately forgive yourself for the times that it just reflexively (oops!). Resolve to forgive yourself. Go beyond forgiveness and just unconditionally accept that you are divine perfection. This keeps your heart open when platitudes fail.

Here is how you can positively align with the **Water** Elemental: Feel unconditionally, heal unresolved trauma by loving it and setting it free, say nothing, listen more, give someone your full attention and zero judgment, grow your intuition by practicing it, listen to animals/plants/minerals, unconditionally love, receive unconditional love, when you feel everything let it go in love.

When we align with the Elementals, we offer ourselves a glorious chance to be in our bodies and to fuel them with inspiration and love. When that does not happen in the ways that we like it to, we often negatively align with the **Water** Elemental like this:

We cannot hear people; no empathy; we forget how to take care of ourselves and others; no intimacy; an inability to identify with anything besides our own pain; denial; addiction; fearful; doubting; and no resolve to improve ourselves.

Man is that gloomy. Let's change that around.

Ways to Positively Align with the Water Elemental:

1. Open your heart.

2. Open your heart again.

3. Keep opening your heart every day and every night. It's true, your feelings will get hurt—probably every day. However, it is not true that closing your heart helps. All that does is reject love. And love is the way we heal our hurts. So open your heart.

4. Welcome your sixth sense. Practice it more. Guess what people are going to say to you before they say it. Predict what people will order in restaurants. Find innocuous ways to be in the flow of what's happening that you could not logically expect or know in advance.

5. Feel every feeling, then let it go.

6. When you are emotional, get creative. Write poetry. Sing. Paint. You get the idea; now dance with it.

7. Freely nurture someone just because you can. Rescue a puppy.

8. Honor your family, even if you don't get along with them. Thank them for making it possible for you to be here now.

9. Telepathy is the common language on this planet. Practice it. Talk with a stone; listen to a flower.

10. Drink more clear enlivening water.

11. Shower, bathe, swim in fresh, enlivening water. Savor every moment.

Helloooooooooo Air Elemental!

We like to say that **Air** puts the mental in Elemental. With **Earth**, we enter the bodies. With **Fire**, we inspire the body with unlimited creativity and change. In **Water**, we adore it just because it is. In **Air**, we talk about it, we think about it, we agree upon words so that we can have ways to tell others about what we are learning. **Air** gives us a chance to share as much as possible to as many beings as possible. After all, what is the thing that we are all sharing right now, this second, and every second? We are breathing **Air**.

Here are ways we positively align with the **Air** Elemental: Learning; honest curiosity; childlike newness; mediation; harmony; timeliness; affirming our true natures; balance; prana; speaking up even when it is difficult; diversity; individuality and equality at once; logic; relationships; freedom.

Here are ways you might negatively align with the **Air** Elemental: Being stuck in old patterns; aging unnecessarily; inflexibility; overly logical; lack of imagination; no perspective; shallow breath or not breathing evenly and regularly; overly active mind; thoughts dominating all parts of being; too talkative; not speaking up truthfully; overly obsessed with minutiae; pedantic; refusal to learn.

Ways to Live with the Air Elemental Positively:

1. Breathe.

2. Breathe again, and again. Vary your breath. Find ways to work with different patterns of breathing to awaken different parts of the brain.

3. Whenever possible, consciously insert a breath before acting. This introduces more options, some of which you may not have encountered any other way.

4. Cultivate beginner's mind.

5. Learn from every person and situation.

6. Affirm what a good job you are doing of being you.

7. Affirm what a good job everybody else is doing of being perfectly themselves. Speak up every time you can affirm life and its wonders.

8. Be on time.

9. Follow the rules that sensibly honor and guide life.

10. Speak up spontaneously and respectfully for truth.

11. Even when there is nothing else between you and someone else, respectfully agree to disagree.

That is the four physical Elementals. When you are grounded and present, you can positively align with them over and over. When you are not grounded (not in your body, not here on planet Earth, not present) it is challenging to gracefully integrate the Elementals. Start your Elemental aligning with grounding your body and fueling it with their loving gifts.

Welcome to the Ethers Elemental!

Time to align with the **Ethers**! Now we are in a new dimension, literally. The **Ethers** host the physical and the beyond-physical realms of life. If you didn't pause and do a fun and honoring ritual before the other Elementals, now is the time. Stop. Enhance lifeforce unimaginably. We will be here when you get back.

Here are some ways that you might positively express the **Ethers** Elemental: stillness; full conscious awareness; connecting to your guides/totems/angels/Spirits; meditation; visualization; freely uniting with all life; practicing unconditional love and acceptance; peace at the core; enlightenment; accepting what you do not know or understand; healing; evolution; acting upon your multidimensionality—in other words, be your own Super Hero! Revel in that and affirm it and come up with your own ways of joining with the **Ethers** lovingly. Simultaneously recognize some of the ways that you can negatively express the **Ethers** Elemental: Escapism; consistent ungroundedness; refusal to adapt to situations and to others; judgment; separation; mistrust; lack; co-dependency; martyrdom; wishing others ill; negative attachments; unforgiving; obsession; inability to express your power positively.

Ways to Live the Ethers Positively now:

1. Any conscious movement. Yoga, Tai Chi, etc.

2. Intent. Whenever you consciously and respectfully utilize lifeforce, you are embodying your Spirit.

3. Talk to your Spirit families and Guides. Get to know them. Don't just ask them for what you want. Become friends because you freely choose to do so.

4. Be in charge of your life. Accept your ability to respond to everything and anything.

5. Consciously choose joy. Even when that is hard it will grow more life, more possibilities and more love.

6. Detach. Freely let go of expectations. Just experience the gift of now.

7. Find the gift in everything. Insist upon it. Expand your gifts.

8. Have fun. Whenever you do what really pleases you, your soul is grateful and pleased.

9. Study other philosophies and wise ways.

10. Practice being multidimensional. It doesn't matter if you don't know what that is. Who does? Just find a way. Practice will do the rest.

11. Trust.

Aligning with the **Ethers** simultaneously grounds all of the physical Elementals within you and around you. When you feel out of balance with any of the Elements breathe with that Elemental until your energy harmonizes itself or meditate with the **Ethers** until you are integrating unconditional love and acceptance.

Note: the qualities of the Elementals listed here are suggested jumping-off places. Familiarize yourself with them in the ways that most speak to you. Those are the true Elemental qualities.

For us, we simply observe how each Elemental dances in Nature. When we want to work with **Fire**, we watch the Sun or we light a candle and see how it changes its world. Every Elemental speaks to every human being just a little differently. When we are listening to Elementals in their own habitat we immediately hear their invitations to join with them and how to join with them. Aligning with the Elementals and our Elemental Birth Imprint is a life long conversation and co-creation. We are eternally grateful.

Finding your Elemental Birth Imprint

We never found our Elemental Birth Imprints, they found us. Each day we listen to the Spirits around us, especially Nature Spirits, and they guide us down wise paths that maybe we couldn't have found otherwise. That is when Grandmother Sweet Shield appeared. We found each other unexpectedly for us, and right on time, according to her. She is our Spiritual Grandmother. We speak together every day and she always directed us to living with the Elementals. Grandmother always invites us to embrace life at the core. It was after we had been balancing our own Elementals with breath, color, movement, sound and freedom, that Grandmother told us about Elemental Birth Imprints.

Then, she told us our Elemental Birth Imprints and it was glorious. Still is. It allows us to face life beyond the judgments of our personalities. It urges us to simply be with life just as we really are, just as we were before we learned separation.

We approach every situation through our Elemental Birth Imprint first. It does not limit us but simply shows us our core learnings and healing. We know that the **Water** and **Fire** in our own personal Elemental Birth Imprints will continually attract emotional circumstances. On a day full of hope and wonder we know this means that whatever we feel we can heal. When we are down on ourselves, that emotionality feels depressing and defensive. Either way, Grandmother says, "You will heal. That much is inevitable." So we stay with it and we consciously choose for our Elemental Birth Imprints to lead to our wholeness. It is a path to union that ultimately we have never left and never will leave.

Aren't you excited now to know your Elemental Birth Imprint? Everybody is. We share Elemental Birth Imprints when the other person agrees to be fully and respectfully responsible for their own Elemental Birth Imprint information and its honoring. Once that permission is given, we hear Grandmother whisper that specific 2-leggeds Elemental Birth Imprint in our ears.

It isn't our intuition. It is comes from our listening. And it is something different that is continually evolving. Grandmother Sweet Shield says, "In this time between the Ages, willingness is everything. Whatever willingness you show your Spirit, it matches, and then goes beyond that. In that place of MORE, you are continually invited to grow and to grow you simply have to show even MORE willingness—maybe it is never-ending like true life. If you keep coming up with more willingness that you offer your Spirit, then the ways you come together change. It goes from questions and answers to a conversation. You meet in a place so beyond need and desire that anything can happen and does. You are equals and then everything is simply open to you. Any questions that you have, have already been answered. You are the answer. That is where you will find your Elemental Birth Imprint. It comes to you because it cannot <u>not</u> come to you."

For us, Elemental Birth Imprints live beyond intuition. They just are who we are and they come to us when we are ready. We have not yet figured out a way to tell other people how to find their Elemental Birth Imprints on their own—at least not yet. So we listen to Grandmother and we pass on Elemental Birth Imprints when willingness and Now come together perfectly.

Next, we want to tell you what we have heard from Grandmother about the most basic combinations of Elemental Birth Imprints.

Earth Elemental Birth Imprints

The most common Imprints have two Elementals. The second most common Imprint has only one Elemental. Whichever Elemental is first is the one that you came to planet Earth to learn the most about and focus upon and to integrate wholly. The second Elemental acts as the m.o. for the first; it is <u>how</u> you express what you have come here to be and to heal.

Earth and **Earth/Earth** Elemental Birth Imprints: These Elemental Birth Imprints ask you to appreciate landing upon the Earth. A lot of good folks with this Elemental Birth Imprint don't yet feel like they belong but they crave it. They want to act in beauty and within the natural cycles of things. When they are in balance, they do just that. Nobody can pull them off their center. Sometimes they seem more like a crystal or a plant or a 4-legged than a human. They innately spring from their instincts and respond to life fully.

This is not always popular with humans who are distracted or lured by glamour alone. Yet a willing, evolving **Earth** Elemental Birth Imprint understands innately that they have their own perfect worth that cannot be judged poorly by anybody, even themselves. From this full comfort in their own skin, they give and receive easily, simply, graciously.

When they are out of balance, **Earth** Elemental Birth Imprints dislike everything. They forget how to connect, how to belong. Some chase after material goods alone, trying to fill up their lack. Others stay disconnected. None of their efforts are sustained enough to connect them with the flow of life again. Many times they become depressed and diseased.

Ways for Earth Elemental Birth Imprints to Balance Themselves

No matter what, **Earth** Elemental Birth Imprints are invited to take full responsibility for their lives. When they choose to be the masters of their own destinies, the captains of their own souls, they land surely and gracefully in their own bodies. Then they have resources and gifts aplenty to respectfully manifest whatever they need and want.

Earth Elemental Birth Imprints must cultivate a life-long conversation with the Earth Mother and Her seasons.

For double **Earth** Elemental Birth Imprints (or **Earth/Earth**) it probably sounds confusing to have an **Earth/Earth** imprint. Why wouldn't it just be an **Earth** imprint? The single Elemental Imprints possess a tremendous focus. They innately eliminate distraction or options from what they choose to do. With a double Elemental Imprint, there is greater flexibility. There is an ability to utilize the Elementals to play off of each other for more perspective and variety. For instance, an **Earth** Elemental Birth Imprint tends to find the things she/he likes—that works for him/her—and stick with them with amazing resiliency or stubbornness—their choice.

A double **Earth** Elemental Birth Imprint uses a whole spectrum of different Earth qualities and lets them play off of (or fight with) the other qualities for their greatest healing.

A double **Earth** generally is fascinated by his/her body and is curious about how things work. When this person positively aligns with the **Earth** Elemental, they bring calm and steadiness to any situation, even crisis. This person then automatically learns from everything and can offer wisdom about anything. One of the things they most admire is loyalty. When you are kind to them, they are generous and abundant.

When the double **Earth** is out of synchronization, it keeps to itself excessively. This person finds it hard to trust anything. Instead of their usual beauty and grace, they are awkward and listless. When angry, they become stubborn.

Earth/Fire Imprint

Here we find beings who at the core want to bring something grand, magnificent, lavish, to life—to everyday life. They own dreams. Visions stalk them regularly. When they are in balance, energy flows through them easily, regularly and constantly. They burst with energy and tremendous stamina to focus it, to wield it. **Earth/Fire** beings know how to translate the magic of all dimensions to this reality and the magic of this reality to all dimensions. They speak fluently in real-world magnificence.

When out of balance, they cannot connect the bigness of their energy with the "smallness" of their bodies. They tend to judge things immediately and negatively: "That will never work." "No one ever helps me." "I'll never be able to do what I really want." Then their energy comes in unmanageable explosions of anger and impatience; nothing happens fast enough or big enough. Other times they cannot ground their lifeforce and creativity. All the splendor of their visions seems to ride right past them without stopping. They can then feel depressed, disconnected and alone.

So let's happily ground Earth/Fire:
1. Conscious continual movement—these beings must be in their bodies and fuel them regularly and generously. Otherwise their creativity and visions will sputter; they will die off without fuel.

2. Sun and warmth—it helps to heat up their bodies: sauna, exercise and summertime sunshine do the job nicely.

3. Support teams—if you have this Imprint, surround yourself with patient, loyal friends and associates who can bridge between the bigness of your dreams and the minutiae of what makes them so in the world.

4. All-out optimism and good cheer—people with this Imprint are often told that they can't have everything they want. Whenever possible and sane, they should not compromise. They breathe, they live to hold the space for the biggest possibilities this species has ever known, and more. It's true, not ALL of their dreams will come true—they are not meant to do so. Sometimes their spectacular visions are just supposed to breed other visions that are a little more logical. These will come true and forever grow bigger, brighter potentials.

Earth/Fire beings: Listen to your hearts and love the bigness of your visions and nurture them wisely.

Earth/Water

These beings are here on the Earth for healing. There are many definitions for healing. When we use it here it means utterly caring for your own lifeforce - to feel and release unconditionally all hurt trauma and struggle. Whenever that is occurring, these beings have more lifeforce and love that keeps healing themselves and simultaneously holding the space for others to do the same for themselves as they wish. In our world, ('Twintreess') we can only truly heal ourselves. As we interact with others, the most healing we can offer is to be fully whole and hold the space unconditionally for them to heal themselves.

Earth/Water loves celebrating the natural flows of life and the Earth. In balance, they bring peace, empathy and respondability to every situation no matter what. Whether they realize it consciously or not, they model themselves after the Earth Mother: generously offering any gifts they can in just the right moment. They can be quite sensual and profoundly appreciative of the natural world.

When these beings are out of balance they are hyper sensitive and feel hurt by others even when that was not intended. They do not share their open hearts and can instead become gloomy, struggling and lonely.

To cheer up an Earth/Water being:

1. Play with crystals, plants, food and baby animals - the cycles of new and precious life endear themselves to their own Spirit and gifts, all over again.

2. Have some regular dependable routines—rituals at important times of the day, night, and season. Meditate at sunrise. Visualize just before bedtime. Camp out during the Equinox. **Earth/Water** absorbs the innate power of certain seasons and times of the Earth.

3. Garden—grow things and grow your own contentment simultaneously.

4. Family—be as loving with your family as possible, even if you do not get along with them. And, if it is not in your best interest to be around them, make new family. Love them. Nourish each other.

Note: This is a symbiotic Elemental Birth Imprint. As such, it will flow easily with all kinds of energy. In balance, it exponentially manifests enduring wonders. Out of balance, it will disrupt helpful patterns of life regularly.

Earth/Air

These beings are born ready to learn. They open themselves with great curiosity and strong powers of observation. They enjoy watching and connecting the cycles of life. Perhaps more than anything they crave to understand and to be understood.

When these people harmoniously integrate **Earth/Air** they tend to be life-long teachers/students. The world fascinates them. They look for the underlying patterns and explanations of everything so that they can predict the movements of life. And while they love to explore, they also love a safe and comfortable home from which they can study and share their expertise with the world.

When **Earth/Air** react negatively to life they tend towards being know-it-alls or purposefully withholding helpful information. One of their greatest judgments is, "That is not fair!" If someone or something does not strictly adhere to their specific morality, they will dismiss them. They lose their inherent objectivity and instead lead with judgmental rules that do not honor or fit the people or situations around them. They must watch out for stubbornness or they will forget their natural curiosity and pioneering.

How to integrate Earth/Air consciously:

1. Keep learning. If you continually study anew you will stay young yet wise.

2. Speak up respectfully for what you know—this Imprint can remember anything. It understands reason and logic and dovetails them with practicality. When they kindly share their resources no one has to needlessly re-invent the wheel.

3. Harmonize between spontaneity and regularity—to build on a positive foundation, this Imprint likes to learn and then record and organize information. It soothes and supports them to regularly witness themselves and life and report it somehow. Simultaneously it reinvigorates them to periodically put away their notes and dance on the mountaintop - to do something marvelously and unexpectedly silly and wake up that inner child.

Earth/Ethers

(Note: **Ethers** are rare in any Imprints.)

These beings remember their truth and destinies earlier than most. They come with a profound sense of mission and begin manifesting it as soon as possible. Have you ever seen an old soul child? While they can't talk to you yet, everything about them speaks volumes. They "know" what is happening. It's undeniable. You know that they know because inherently they can communicate anything, anywhere, anytime.

When **Earth/Ethers** express themselves harmoniously they offer everyone and anything relentless patience and acceptance. No matter what happens they are ready to respond. They deal with it. They deal with it calmly, kindly, and as immediately as possible. While they do not often move hurriedly, their bodies flow in even, timely grace. They seem to pull miracles out of thin air.

When **Earth/Ethers** cannot harmoniously integrate their Imprint, they rail at the injustices of the world. They obsess. They keep score of every lack and struggle, and unfortunately for all, they remember everything. Even when it's not helpful they speak with a certainty that convinces others of half truths.

If **Earth/Ethers** cannot engage unconditionally with the world they drop out. They stop finding anything lovely or loving about life and they isolate themselves. Once they do this, it is difficult to get them to return to love, meaning and joy.

To integrate Earth/Ethers positively:

1. Find your guides. This Imprint must connect to a higher power or become discombobulated and disenchanted. However, if they regularly speak to their Spirit families and allies, they hold the space for body/Spirit union without pause.

2. Mentor others. Wisdom and awareness come easily to these people. If they continually share it unconditionally they are happily interwoven with life; everything has meaning, purpose and they align with that profoundly.

3. Retreat—plan regular times away from noise and distraction. These do not have to be long big trips. However, they ought to be regular ones. At least meditate every day and save a day for silence. Shut off the phone and the world regularly. Walk in nature. Listen and renew in the stillness.

4. The middle path—it is natural for this Imprint to respond to dramatic cycles of life. When needed, they help in a crisis and they persevere long past all others. To prepare for these callings, this being must consider regular ever-changing activities. Sometimes they must be utterly still. Other times they must push themselves physically, emotionally and psychically past their limits. And, amongst all of this, they must connect with the middle path. Find balance. Stay with it. Honor your awareness of it.

Fire

Fire Elemental Birth Imprints live and breathe as large as possible. They inherently connect with life. They give and receive energy powerfully. To keep moving and growing they hold a vision bigger than themselves and they do not like to ever let it go—"the Don Quixote's of the world." When they are in synch with lifeforce they change profoundly and regularly. They love to move wherever the winds blow them. They trust in a bigger picture knowing that logic will not be the final determining factor in their stories. They dream enthusiastically and if you ask them about it they will tell you everything with bright colors and loud music.

When this Imprint is out of synch with life, it will mistrust everything. It will not understand what is happening and everything alarms it. It finds it difficult to start new ventures—any new ventures, even getting out of bed. This person will sound suspicious, regretful and determinately unhappy.

To wake up a Fire Imprint:

Shout at the top of your lungs in their face, "I LOVE YOU, YOU WILD CRAZY PERSON!" Of course, this would be a last ditch effort so let's intervene in less drastic measures first . . .

1. Cultivate enthusiasm like you would your garden—identify your passions and feed them regularly, even on the days you don't want to, and, especially, do it then. It is much easier to restart a **Fire** when you have warm embers left.

2. Transform everything. Stop fearing change. Move. Change careers. Cut your hair. Most of all change your habits. Find your unpredictable streak and nurture it.

3. Be an artist. Creativity thrills you. Find what you love and do it as if it were an art form. Do it eloquently to the nth degree and perfect your art work happily each day.

4. Happy, happy, happy—even if it makes you crazy some days (and it will), immerse yourself in ready joy. Plaster the walls with happy pictures, posters and sayings. Do affirmations all day long. Sing. Dance. Joke with people that laugh non-stop. Find everything you can celebrate and do so continually. When you don't feel like partying find at least one small way to create a party. Pizza frequently.

Fire/Fire

One time we told a new mother (at her request) that her new baby was a **Fire/Fire**. She gasped. There is something about **Fire/Fire** that launches out unpredictably; it cannot be corralled or understood. **Fire/Fire** beings ever look to the Stars. These people are born on the mountaintop. They survey life from the largest perspectives and then they spend the rest of their time climbing higher mountains to see what is next. They crave relentless inspiration. And when they have even the smallest bit of it, they smile. They find joy in a mud puddle.

When these beings are living in balance they change themselves inside out constantly. They may not show it yet they continually observe themselves. They learn from their own motivations and when they understand them, they shift them. They like to move things so that they can change from what is possible to what is impossible and so on and so on. They instinctively mistrust limits. They like testing themselves against them. Why walk when you can fly!

When **Fire/Fire** beings live out of synch with themselves, they can be rash. They can risk things unnecessarily and change things before the results are in to be measured. This impulsiveness makes them and others jumpy. They find it difficult to stay still long enough to be as intimate, open hearted, and as generous as they truly are. They naturally tend to be childlike, yet when they are not evolving they act childishly.

Calm down and ground magnificently with Fire/Fire:

1. Variety. Always keep the widest variety of activities, projects and possibilities available. This being can be afraid of boredom because it believes it will find out that life is meaningless at the core. These people must keep fueling their prodigious trust and interconnection with a benevolent universe. They need to be able to do anything, anywhere, anytime.

2. Pure food and drink. These people live for energy. It is simply common sense that they must fuel themselves with natural, organic, and simple food and drink. And if their metabolism demands it, feast frequently. Use only high quality clean pure water.

3. Continual movement. **Fire/Fire** must ground. Their change and creativity must root in their bodies, first, in order to produce what they choose in the world.

4. A cause. **Fire/Fire** beings want to BELIEVE. They must breathe it in every moment. Encourage them to devote themselves to at least one profound cause constantly. It will not deplete their energy. It will alchemically grow it.

5. Friends. The **Fire/Fire** likes to be around people when there is a lot to do together; yet, even when there is not a special occasion these people must stay in touch with the real world through kind and patient friends. Otherwise, they lose touch with reality.

Fire/Earth

These people live to bring the good news to the masses. More than anything, they want many happy endings. Yet, when the fairy tale does not work out, they are not easily perturbed. Instead, those stories become their missions. They will work and work at what needs to be done and whenever possible they will look for transcendent joy to land upon them and others. In balance, they stand up for what they believe and they bring together passion and sweat. Their emotions are dramatic and continually in flux. Even when they are afraid, they consider their fear a healthy challenge. It's all part of their game and they plan to WIN. When push comes to shove, they do neither. Instead, they create miracles out of dust.

When **Fire/Earth** is out of sorts, it rages, it says the first thing that comes, and inevitably, it is brutal. It will fight and fight long past the point of opposition. In short, it does not know how to channel unexpected, sometimes explosive energies productively. When that finally exhausts him/her, s/he has no reserves.

To inspire and re-energize Fire/Earth:

1. Diet. Perhaps of all the two Element Birth Imprints, **Fire/Earth** ought to look to well thought out and continually researched nutrition. While many of them enjoy the buzz of fast food, it erodes their generosity, passion and stamina. It behooves them to care for their digestion.

2. Philosophy/Rituals/Spirituality. These people must have something worthwhile to believe in and to act upon every day of their life.

3. Color. Instinctively, a full range of colors (especially bright ones) cures them of stress and dis-ease.

4. Children. In one way or another, newness brightens them immeasurably. Children in some form (and this can simply be the products of their creativity) makes them smile endlessly.

5. Humor. Laughing yoga was invented for these people. Keep at the ready a constant arsenal of comics, funny DVD's, cute sayings, funny pictures and jokes. This will keep their bodies from taking on too much of the stress of the world.

Fire/Water

These people carry the extremes of emotion. It is their nature to be present with lots of people or one person. They are both dynamic and quiet. When they do speak their heart guides them perfectly.

When **Fire/Water** acts harmoniously they give anyone everything they have: dreams; motivation; optimism; intuitive guidance; faith; and ultimately, lots of presence. They own an endless stream of solutions to all difficulties. When they care for themselves as well as others nothing is impossible. They like big projects (probably the biggest projects!) that will help others. They care for one and all yet they are brave enough to detach whenever necessary.

When **Fire/Water** acts inharmoniously they easily get overwhelmed. They drown in their own stress and cannot find a way out. Then they become needy or distant - whatever their overactive defenses can manipulate the most immediately. Because they run on emotions, they can withdraw into their own worlds where everything they do or feel can be immediately and vociferously justified.

How to balance a Fire/Water:

1. Different kinds of stimuli/people. Here is energy in a full emotional spectrum. To stay healthy and contributing they must expose themselves to many points of view, ideas and beliefs.

2. A beautiful home. At their core, **Fire/Water** will go anywhere, do anything, at least once. And when they have risked themselves so bravely they need to come home to a grounding, calming and regenerative oasis. While they may change their space constantly, they shouldn't live in chaos too long. Keep the home organized, clear, simple and safe. This grounds them.

3. Meditation. **Fire/Water** can spike an emotional graph up and down and sideways all in a nano-second. While some of that stimulates and invigorates, some of it wears down the body's immune system and reserves. They need constant meditation to center themselves in their dramatic world. If possible, align with meditation that has no words or no agenda, just a haven of emptiness.

4. Sensory input—they need a multi-sensory approach to life. Fill their homes with fresh flowers, cushy chairs, both bright and soft lighting, and every kind of music. They crave to be touched in every way. Constant therapeutic massage and bodywork will open up their natural deep wells of wisdom and healing.

5. Practice. Moody? Yes! **Fire/Water** may have invented that state of being. Yet, even they can get bored by it quickly. To keep them healthy, cultivate regular worthwhile practices: volunteer work; Chi Gong; art work; therapy—anything that holds unlimited belief and love. The key is that the practice must be REGULAR, daily at least. It centers them in a dangerously shifting world.

Fire/Air

Unlimited is their domain. They want to be Super Heroes and they can't find any reason not to be. They live and breathe visions. Newness feeds them. They enjoy inspiration for inspiration's sake and if you catch their passion they share it for your sake too.

Fire/Air goes forth boldly and quickly to test out new theories and be excellent pioneers. They blaze new paths and are generous with what they know and their enthusiasm for what can be. **Fire/Air** in balance likes everyone. They invite everybody to the dance. They are happiest when everyone has a chance to do what they truly want. In their world, they expect nothing less.

When **Fire/Air** is out of balance they create their own world where no one actually lives, not even themselves. They can change anything yet have no stick-to-itiveness to create anything worthwhile. While they can learn and remember anything, when they are defensive they remember only part of the facts and manipulate them as they choose.

To balance Fire/Air:

1. Create a spontaneous space to talk about all feelings. While they have easy transpersonal perspectives, there is more difficulty cultivating empathy.

2. Slow down. Doing things as slowly as possible helps to heal the body and the consequences of actions. This encourages care instead of carelessness.

3. Breathing. **Fire/Air** can achieve much if they consciously breathe before doing anything.

4. Mono-tasking. While they can do or at least plan anything, they need to learn to do tasks to the nth degree. Look for ways to care for the big picture and all the details simultaneously.

5. Stones and Crystals. Most **Fire/Air** have more ideas than they can ever give homes to comfortably. Stones and Crystals are the bones of form, the core of manifestation. When **Fire/Air** teams with them they offer energy and passion to <u>grounded</u> co-creation.

Fire/Ethers

These beings hardly seem human. They move in other worlds with a focus so keen everyday people and matters do not always understand. They live in their most idealized world. There, they are clear about their priorities and that what they do is for all. In balance, **Fire/Ethers** live multi-dimensionally. They realize there are many levels of consequences to what they do. They spend their time visioning the most helpful systems, philosophies, and practices that will simultaneously benefit all.

Out of balance, **Fire/Ethers** people are afraid. They do not easily accept responsibility for their gifts so they do not share them. They can become addicted to illusions that cannot find manifestation in the real world. They dissipate vast energies on scattered pursuits and sometimes disillusionment.

Ways to ground Fire/Ethers:

1. Listening. They need to listen to others to learn real perspectives. Simultaneously, they must be listened to also. When someone else recognizes the truth of what they say, they are able to keep creating and refining their profound vision.

2. Healing. Most **Fire/Ethers** innately know the natural order of things. Through constant observation, they can understand how a being functions at its best. When they apply this to themselves, they spontaneously see how and where to feel and heal their own unresolved traumas. They possess innate perspectives to objectively restore themselves to union and vitality.

3. Leadership. Channeling their awesome energies is key to the life and satisfaction of **Fire/Ethers**. While they have little patience to carry out all of their visions, they excel at delegating to trusted others. If they stay in an objective, higher perspective they can monitor the growth of anything worthwhile and foster its kind development.

4. Walking. **Fire/Ethers** must feel their roots and their toes on the Earth. When they remember their bodies they develop empathy that enriches everyone's lives. Walking deliberately helps them discharge rapid, dramatic, ever changing emotions harmlessly and continually.

Water

This Imprint likes living quietly feeling things in its own way, moment to moment. **Water** Imprints BE much more than they DO. Yet, when you need someone to hold your hand they come alive. They feel what you feel and they let you know that. They identify with you and there is little space (or boundaries) between them and anything else. Thinking can be a foreign experience, like a second language they never quite master. However, they tend to natural telepathy and understand beyond words.

In balance, **Water** nurtures and cares for everything, especially new undeveloped things. Being sensitive themselves, they sense vulnerabilities in others and protect quickly. When they turn their empathy inward, they understand their own motivations and, chameleon-like, can change to anything required by their environment.

Water Imprints out of balance obsess about every emotion. All is dramatic and they cannot prioritize in healthy ways. This over-stimulates their defenses continually until they react to everything as a threat, until they are sickly and unable to care for themselves well.

Ways to positively integrate the Water Imprint:

1. Intimate relationships. These people know how to bond as deeply as anyone and need this in return. They crave being listened to or understood without judgment. Unconditional partners and family steady their lives.

2. Channeling nurturance. For these people to develop positive self esteem they need to lavish care on others who can unconditionally accept it.

3. Time to simply BE. Emotions run a **Water** Imprint's life. And emotions cannot run on clock or calendar time. **Water** Imprints must have regular timeless, unstructured space just to be. They are so good at feeling everything and everyone else, they must schedule time and space to take off all feelings and simply know their own thoughts and emotions. This is how they know their own hearts.

4. Silence. **Water** Imprint people can be extra sensitive to ALL stimuli. It is important for them to have less noise and scattering distractions so that they can feel their own truth easily.

Water/Water

These people live surrounded by emotions so thoroughly that they permeate every thought, act and moment. They instinctively know how all beings of the Earth belong to each other. They feel the cycles of all things rise and fall in our blood and our most basic natures. While they may not be overly enamored of words, they appreciate any way that allows everyone to be understood and included. They almost always identify with children and animals. When in balance, they can feel their cracks in their Shields by offering unconditional love non-stop. With priorities that center around nurturance, receptivity and sensitivity, the **Water/Water** beings' presence supports all of us moving slower, gentler in greater awareness. **Water/Water** people intuitively embody "no child left behind."

Out of balance, **Water/Water** becomes so vulnerable to everything they shut down. They close off empathy and either form their own cold worlds or become martyrs and co-dependent. They can so lack initiative in the everyday world that they do not attract the listening and understanding they need at the core. Hence, they will then judge most people as being either uncaring or obsessively needy.

To balance Water/Water:

1. Nature. Get in nature as often as possible. The Earth Mother instinctively helps ground emotions.

2. Mentor children. By supporting and caring for kids, **Water/Water** finds the true qualities of life that they value.

3. Art. Cultivate other languages besides words to express all there is unconditionally.

4. Regular exercise. **Water/Water** people can be overwhelmed by the tides of emotions. They lose themselves and don't realize that they have a choice in how they personally will live in that much water. Regular movement will ground excess emotion and bring back renewing cycles of regeneration.

Water/Earth

These fluid, gentle beings fit in with anywhere. They aspire to this. They want to belong so that they can give and receive as generously as life bestows upon them. They embody gratitude. From this they flower into natural fertility, and contentment. In balance, they move with an inner directed grace and ease. They align with the cycles of the Earth and the Moon and their bodies know this. When they explore their own psyches they are richly rewarded. They revel in being alive without unnecessary rationalization, judgment or agendas.

Out of balance, **Water/Earth** people avoid feelings and connecting to anything. Their bodies grow sluggish and sometimes swell with unprocessed feelings/fluids. They go from day to day listlessly and feel justified in doing so, "That's just the way things are." They get stuck in ruts and almost nothing changes or uplifts them.

How to Positively Express the Water/Earth Imprint:

1. Enthusiasm. Find what makes you really happy and do it and do it and do it. The more joyful you are, the more naturally and spontaneously and exponentially you grow that for all.

2. Plan unexpected activities. Spontaneous change can be the greatest ally for this Imprint.

3. Food. Eat slowly, consciously and savor it precisely. Sometimes this Imprint abuses the sensations of food and/or becomes addicted to it. When you are an equal partner with the magic and the alchemy of food you release unhealthy dependence.

4. Support team! Surround yourself with happy steady friends. You need regular social contact to grow and to share the treasures you innately possess.

5. Journal. Record your deepest feelings and thoughts so that you can learn from them without judgment. Not everyone will be able to be as intimate as you so you need to be intimate with yourself. Be your own best friend and resolve to be utterly truthful with yourself about everything. Remember when you go deeply into your feelings that everything is a cycle. This too shall pass.

Water/Fire

This Imprint expresses unlimited undifferentiated lifeforce. It inherently accepts a core divine order and doesn't always need to define or explain it. While these people can be dynamic and creative they do not always translate to others though they try. In balance, **Water/Fire** wants to care for the world. They like seeing everybody happy even though they don't expect it. They go with the flow and simultaneously they want to improve it, make it more efficient. They adore change and can reinvent themselves top to bottom continually.

Out of balance, **Water/Fire** quickly judges and loses patience and empathy. They demand that others change to get what feels right yet are incapable of defining what that means. Then, they become overwhelmed and surrender to skepticism, doubt and disillusionment.

Ways to Ground and Integrate Water/Fire:

1. Creativity. Provide open and undefined space to express constant feelings and ever moving lifeforce.

2. Grounding. Whatever practices you can do daily to be in the body, do them. Appreciate your health and movement.

3. Nurture. Directly learn from the movement and patterns in nature. Your telepathy is strong. Encourage it. Talk to the Earth and all Her children.

4. Center Stillness. Go to that core quiet within. Have no agenda, needs or expectation. Simply absorb the Center Stillness. Be at home with yourself.

5. Connecting to your Spirit. Keep listening for the small Spirit whispers. Get really familiar with them. You need a continually bigger brighter perspective from which to look at life and to be.

Water/Air

You want to balance yin and yang and all ways of being and doing. Yes! Once you do balance (a constant juggling) you learn and love to translate this to others. In your heart you feel that everyone ought to have the opportunity to be enlightened. You often take this on as your mission. When you do this, you deeply appreciate both the uniqueness and commonalities of all people.

In balance, you feel what everybody is feeling and are able to put words to it. You take what is deep in the hearts, lighten it, make it easier to understand and accept. Many **Water/Air** Imprints are teachers of some kind. You feel almost obligated to share what is important for all.

Out of balance, **Water/Air** Imprints judge and do not know that they do so. Sometimes you are too quick and to shallow with assessments. You proclaim, "I am speaking from my heart," yet sometimes it is only the defenses talking. You want to be as intimate and as loving as possible with everyone but when this cannot happen you isolate yourself even if it does not look to be that way from the outside.

Ways to Harmonize the Water/Air Imprint:

1. Vary the types of contacts. It is important for this Imprint to be around people; however, to truly learn and grow it supports greatly if you are around many different kinds of people continually. This way, you can continually broaden your perspective and ultimately know yourself better in those reflections.

2. Walking in nature. Get your lungs and body pumping. Walk in remote countryside or wilderness and really drink in the fresh air.

3. Solitude. **Water/Air** people have lots of feelings and lots of thoughts and just need personal time to sort them; otherwise your mind says the same things over and over.

4. Truth-telling. You are diplomatic which sometimes means you are not saying everything. Much healing comes from your freely speaking deep emotions so that they can lovingly be accepted and released.

5. Journaling. You need to know yourself. To distinguish your feelings from everyone else's; you may need to record them. This information needs to be at the ready during emotional charged times. It will provide learning and perspective.

Water/Ethers

Words do not demonstrate this Imprint. You long to BE. You appreciate doing what you wish when you feel it the most strongly. And when you feel deeply they are loyal, determined, nurturing and protective. You focus on your families (biological and chosen) and often times feel that loving and taking care of those family members are why you are on the planet.

In balance, this Imprint believes in love. Sometimes nothing else truly exists. Everything that happens is simply another form of love greeting you even when it challenges or hurts. While you are preternaturally aware and sensitive you instinctively know how to stretch beyond hurt feelings to see the healing and yes, more love, making itself available to you and all.

Out of balance, this Imprint dislikes people. You do not understand why humans do not always follow divine and Earth order/seasons naturally. You obsess on the dark side of emotions. You have few friends because you mistrust the motives of all. Because you are incredibly intuitive you can slant this guidance to "prove" that humanity is suspect.

Ways to Positively Channel a Water/Ethers Imprint:

1. Water. Sounds obvious doesn't it? You rely upon clear clean water to let go of the day's activities and emotions. It is crucial to drink enough water all day long to keep positive. It may be even more helpful to shower at the end of the day to let go of everything. If you cannot physically shower, visualize swimming in sweet clarifying water before going to sleep peacefully at night.

2. Speak up! **Water/Ethers** are profound beings. Put words to wisdom. It keeps you clear from bias and it shares great inspirations with others.

3. Running and jumping and playing. **Water/Ethers** need to move until they sweat. Your heart loves a good work-out. It refreshes the body, the blood and the outlook. A stroll in the park won't do it. Really move everything as much and as kindly and as often as possible.

4. Family/Boundaries. This Imprint can look like the saviors in their families. Your innate knowingness is like no one else's. When you speak up, you enlighten darkness that no one else seems willing to do. However if you are always providing this enlightenment, no one will truly grow. It simply fosters co-dependency. After a **Water/Ethers** speaks its heart, s/he ought to walk away for awhile honoring and trusting that everyone else will receive the gift and find their own perfect way in their own perfect timing

5. Let go. Let go of what? If you don't know, just let go. Let go of everything as immediately, as gracefully, as cheerfully, as freely, as continually, as possible. Plan that. If you don't know how to let go, practice. It is such pure freedom you will repeat it with great success. Keep it up.

Air

Secretly every **Air** Imprint person reading this BOOK skipped ahead to this section because it is the most fascinating part. You love to learn, to think, to explore, and to pioneer areas of study. You prefer to be quick and free to change anything. While you don't readily identify with everything you appreciate being able to understand the how's and why's of all. If you can find logic in something you will approve even when what's being done would not be your choice. Perhaps more than anything, you need interaction. You crave as many people and possibilities to learn from and to somehow enjoy as any other Imprint.

In balance, **Air** people stand for freedom and equality. You love seeing everybody get along. At gatherings you talk to everyone. In more intimate settings you help to make sure that every being gets a voice. You love collecting opinions and are not easily offended.

Out of balance, **Air** Imprint people are the loneliest people of all. When you are disillusioned (which thankfully doesn't usually last) you pretend to participate. You easily know how to say the right things but your heart is not available. When you isolate yourself, defenses take over completely repeating their prejudices and hurts obsessively and relentlessly. It becomes hard to truly listen to anything else. If you remain defensive you use your powers of persuasion to delude yourself about reality.

To Balance an Air Imprint:

1. Breathing. Really, this one can/does balance all Elementals in all situations. However, it can be most crucial with an **Air** Imprint because your mind talks so loud that the only thing that can clear this sometimes is focusing on the breath. It is most helpful if you breathe conscious patterns every day that let go of thinking or outcomes.

2. Organization. These Imprints excel at planning and efficiency but usually they focus this skill on others. Bring it home. Make sure to keep your own space clutter-free and respectfully efficient and user-friendly.

3. Martial Arts. Some **Air** Imprints are totally unfamiliar with their bodies. You "think" you know it; however bodies are sensual experiences. Thinking alone literally doesn't touch them. Martial Arts plant you in the body and hone your instincts. It cultivates your considerate and spontaneous awareness. It brings **Air** and Earth together.

4. Safe expression. There is no substitute for talking things out for an **Air** Imprint person. Do it and do it regularly. However when you are needy you can wear out friends and family. Establish respectful boundaries in these situations. Call a professional or have guidelines with friends. Set up time limits where you can rant and rave with harm to none and then let go. These ranting and raving periods are done with mutual permission.

5. Listen. Take the prodigious energy of speaking and thinking and tune it into fully listening. Resist the urge to speak when someone else is talking or seeks your opinion. Hold the space for listening first. Watch what happens. Learn. Clear your mind. Open your heart.

Air/Air

You come to the Earth to heal. While you often practice life fairly easily, your need to know spurs you on relentlessly. You are like a three year old who just learned the word, "why." While you do not plumb the depths of feeling you desperately want to understand. All of your being believes that if you understand you are safe, you are learning, you are helping, you are focusing on light in great darkness. Because you change your mind and opinions regularly, your optimism flourishes. Ultimately you think that all ignorance and struggle will one day end.

In balance, **Air/Air** people use their voices to connect people, places and things. You feel that constantly flowing information will solve almost anything. When learning something new you become so inspired you make it their mission to share it with as many people as possible. You love to explain what you know and to do it in a way that is easily and immediately accessible to all. Your sense of fairness insists upon it.

Out of balance, **Air/Air** people talk excessively; yet they are connecting nothing. You are often distracted and try to act upon less than the whole picture of reality. Even when you need more information to understand, you hurry through everything seeking to avoid discomfort above all. You may joke or smile about your dilemmas but the truth is you cannot or will not plunge into emotions enough to be truly intimate with yourself and life. At this point, nothing will satisfy you and to camouflage this your mind fills with minutiae, distractions and illusions.

To Balance the Air/Air Imprint Person:

1. Meditation. After that, do meditation. After that, meditate continually.

2. Water. Surround yourself in and around water to open your heart. Soak your feet every night before bedtime. Go to a hot springs. Soak in your own tub, and while doing so, disengage from thoughts. While you can't completely stop thinking, just don't engage thoughts; let them come and go without attaching to them. When you can't get in or around water play the sounds of waterfalls, rivers, and the ocean.

3. The Moon. Get to know and love all the phases of the Moon. This speaks to your body naturally and enhances your instincts and awareness beyond thoughts.

4. Move your body. It almost goes without saying that **Air/Air** people tend to live from the neck up. Find movement that exercises every single part of your body. Make it a game.

5. Sing. You possesses impressive communication skills and needs. Channel that creatively. Someone else's songs can unexpectedly activate feelings spontaneously. Sing as loudly and as passionately as possible.

Air/Earth

You love to lighten up life. You explore anything and in reporting great drama you like to find the positive lesson . . . and do it with a twinkle in your eye. You pass down the stories from generation to generation. You remind us that when we don't know our history we are doomed to repeat it boldly. While learning anything you treasure being able to focus on what is practical and immediately efficient. You love problem-solving or at least you feel compelled to use knowledge well and handily. One of your great talents is to refine systems that help humans and the Earth.

In balance, **Air/Earth** loves movement. You adore feeling how your body work and appreciate the satisfaction of hard work. When focused, you will figure out how anything works, especially machines, technology, even institutions. You are not always the front line leader but usually are quick to be the spokesperson and networker.

When out of balance, the **Air/Earth** person obsesses about details. Why? Because you are disappointed your best efforts have not saved the world. So you harp on the little pieces you can control. If anyone joins in this you stand by them. If they do not join in, you will focus on bringing them down and sacrificing the real issue at hand. Your disposition becomes jaded because the pessimism in your mind plays those tapes incessantly and believes them.

To balance Air/Earth:

1. Plan spontaneity. Regularly schedule foolish outings. Be open to little parties on the spur. Let go of seriousness. Be a child. Harmlessly change your habits. When you get dressed today, wear one of every color.

2. Beauty and art. Find a passion that regularly appreciates what is beautiful. If you must obsess about something, let it be gratitude for what is truly lovely.

3. Animals. Live with 4-legged companions as equal members of the family. If you are unable to live with animals, volunteer time at a shelter. Exercise their dogs. Let them steal your heart.

4. Organization versus spontaneity. Use your amazing organizing skills of to help people who truly need it. Yet, when you go home let go of the need to obsess about details. Find fun things to do instead.

5. Am I in harmony with all parts of my being? Spontaneously and regularly ask yourself this question all day long. When you ask it, stop your daily routine, check in with yourself, be open to everything and listen. Are any being ignored? If so, befriend them. Be as good friends with yourself as you are with others.

Air/Fire

This Imprint always stirs things up. You shake your beliefs and question your answers. It is not because you necessarily doubt them. It is because the sharing of ideas always bridges to enlightenment, to utopia. You open your mind to anything and usually find the light, even in dark corners or bizarre circumstances. You love the journey as long as you have someone to share it with and something useful to contribute. You judge nothing, and you will find solutions and then you will dig out new perspectives that render problems as needless.

When in balance, **Air/Fire** delights everyone in the room. You adapt to any person and circumstance immediately. You are a true chameleon. Even in the darkest circumstance you find humor and delight. Nobody knows how you do it. You just do it relentlessly.

When this Imprint is out of balance, it cares for nothing, because you have forgotten how to risk and give and receive intimacy. To you everything is just a game, or numbers, or a theory. Nothing is real because you haven't felt it. While you can still inspire huge groups of people into action, you do nothing. When you are out of harmony you do not even know how to change your self defeating habits. At the core, you have lost faith in yourself.

To Balance the Air/Fire Imprint:

1. Never play with matches.

2. Humor. Couldn't you tell?

3. Slow down. Find at least one passion where you still yourself and focus on beauty. God is in the details. Get to know that so intimately that you can say it and mean it.

4. Tell the truth. It is the easiest path. Honor everybody with the truth. Sometimes you might be too blunt. Practice telling the truth until you are gracious and grateful. You will reap huge rewards. So will everybody else.

5. Hobbies. Find truly worthwhile hobbies that engage all of your creativity. Otherwise you can obsess on immediate gratification and addictions.

6. Inspiring stories. Your words carry more than the average weight (to yourself as well as others). Probably you are a natural storyteller. Focus on the dramatic ones that inspire even the most jaded audiences. If you are going to say things over and over, let it be the story of everyday heroes and magi.

Air/Water

You are inherently versatile. Potentially you were born with many gifts or at least the fluency to switch between multiple ideas, topics, personalities, feelings and inspirations. Deep down you truly care. Even when you are distracted and/or going a mile-a-minute, you know how to shift on a dime. You come back to whatever is truly important, fully and immediately. One of your true talents can be speaking up for those who do not have a ready voice. If you believe in you cause they will stay with it forever.

In balance, you will face any issue and judge nothing. And even when you are afraid, you keep finding ways not to succumb. You know how to regenerate and will help others to do the same.

When out of balance, you live with a vengeance. You choose illusions and delusions and rationalize defending them. While you love to start every day new, full of big dreams, you do not know how to actually "do" anything. You spin your wheels in distractions. At the end of the day, you are so frustrated by what you didn't do, you justify wasting your time over and over again.

How to Balance Air/Water:

1. Just pick something. Start every day with a list of just the very few things you <u>must</u> do. <u>They must be</u> your highest priorities. Then pick one of them and just do it. No matter how many distractions come to you, resolve that you will do this one thing as well as possible. The resulting boost of energy will grow immediately <u>and</u> day after day. You will develop helpful and healthy routines and positive self-esteem.

2. Move regularly. When you don't know what to do or you catch yourself frittering away the day, stop. Let your response be that you will move. Go for a walk. Do Tai Chi. Dance. Do it body and soul. This is what you will bring back to your next activity.

3. Clean your space. While you have many interests and gifts, resist the urge to crowd your home with them. Keep the backdrop of your space simple, quiet and clutter-free. This will innately grow the focus that you are capable of and regularly need.

4. Retreats. Go on retreats regularly, even if they are only minutes long. Take yourself out of stimuli driven environments and just be without an agenda.

Air/Ethers

In any moment, any one of us armed with unconditional absolute willingness can channel greatness. You don't have to own it or understand it. You simply embody it and find a way to give it to others freely. Perhaps nobody does that more readily, more frequently than **Air/Ethers**. We all must find a way—lots of ways—to appreciate that gift. It brings unexpected wisdom when it is truly needed. As you do not always appreciate your own gifts because you are forever open to whatever will work. You come to situations freely, unconditionally and ready to change in a heartbeat. You trust divine timing and are happy to play your part in it.

When in balance, you hold the space for the highest evolution for the human species possible. You see it. You trust in it. In harmony, you act upon it even when you don't understand it. You will unconditionally tell others whatever they need to know to be whole. You can act more like a sacred witness or shamanic guide than any other being. Perhaps it is because you prefer to live in many dimensions at once.

When out of balance, nobody understands a word you say. Even your jokes aren't funny. You can't find simple logic to relate to people with at the appropriate moment. Your incoherency seems to force you into a world of your own, yet it is a highly developed one. Out of harmony, you do not share your gifts as intended.

To Balance an Air/Ethers Imprint:

1. Eat lightly. Rely upon being able to access lots of energy at a moment's notice. This happens simply when you eat light organic food frequently. It maintains a strong metabolism and keeps from bogging down energy in digestion.

2. Good friends. Pick your friends well. Make sure they are unafraid to tell you the truth and simultaneously be supportive. You are inordinately affected by the input and energies of others. Surround yourself with respectful friends and you will ground and center yourself more quickly.

3. Fuel well. **Air/Ethers** likes to absorb energy quickly. Focus on healing yourself single-mindedly and well. Mono-task. When you eat, just savor the food. When you read, give all your attention. When you listen to someone, open your heart, witness it all without judgment. These practices will cut down on distractions to your lifeforce.

4. Sun and skin. At least once a day be naked in the sunlight. Dry brush yourself to release unnoticed accumulations of opinions, philosophies and stimuli. Let the sunlight see what you do not need and burn it away.

5. Silence. Your communications can connect dimensions and miracles. It is important to balance these energetic outputs with periods of silence. Let go of speaking. Let go of thinking. This keeps you fresh, open and free.

Ethers

Ethers is the Element that represents Spirit-moving-in-all-things. You land upon the Earth to bring a consciousness to everything and everyone. You believe with your soul. Everyday existence is not enough for you. You want something transcendent. You seek the new beneath the mundane. You trust that the Spirits in us are perfect in their own ways. In balance, you enjoy the inexplicable. Mystery intrigues you. You are attracted to a unifying philosophy. You appreciate the physical bodies as vessels of immortality and creativity.

Out of balance, the **Ethers** Imprint person finds it difficult to ground into this reality. You feel stifled by its limits and chafe at logic. You find it hard to meet everyday obligations. You crave understanding at the core but don't know how to get it. You want to cultivate trust but are afraid of meaninglessness.

To Balance Ethers:

1. Teachers. Find an honest, dependable teacher in a philosophy that relates respectfully to all parts of life. Follow this wisdom. Give and receive it with others. Connect this with everyday reality.

2. Creativity. Find endless ways to express your creativity. It grows your lifeforce and wonder. It speaks your innate language and sharpens all of your multi-dimensional gifts.

3. Nature. Get out into nature constantly. Let its purity help you drop over-responsibility.

4. Therapeutic bodywork. Regularly receive bodywork that brings together body and Spirit unconditionally. Celebrate this.

5. Facilitate healing. While no one can truly heal anyone besides themselves you can hold the space for others to heal themselves. Support them through affirmations, natural techniques and unconditional acceptance. Create a space where they feel safe and beloved.

Ethers/Ethers

You have a mission. You want to evolve in every way possible. You know it is difficult yet you do not turn away from the challenge. You lean into it. You release expectations and leap into the abyss of the unknown. If others are fortunate enough to be around you, they learn from your profound focus and ability to wield power.

In balance, the **Ethers/Ethers** Imprint appreciates everything. Nothing is too big or too small to be loved. You find beauty and poetry in everything. At the core you are a true romantic. You are in love with all of life and all beings. You see their exquisite potential and hold strong for that to be realized.

Out of balance, the **Ethers/Ethers** Imprint is disappointed by everything. You sense there is more to life yet you cannot access it. You grow overly serious. You try to control everything. Nothing works and even the simplest task will elude you. You flee from responsibility and sometimes suffer profound martyr complexes.

Ways to Balance Ethers/Ethers:

1. Go barefoot.

2. Be constantly sensual. Eat with your fingers. Surround yourself with beautiful things, smells and sounds.

3. Creativity. Be a lifelong artist. Pick at least one art form and master it and then let go of mastery and live it, breathe it, be it. Let beauty bring you meaning and satisfaction.

4. Teach others about the interconnectedness of all life and walk them through living examples of it. Become vibrantly alive together.

Ethers/Earth

You want everything to come together harmoniously, joyfully and utterly. You want to live in a utopia. Not only is that possible, your very existence insists upon it. You gather people together to grow in safe nurturing environments. You model your work after the natural cornucopia of the Earth Mother.

In balance, the **Ethers/Earth** Imprint believes! You believe in fairies, sprites and way beyond Tinkerbell. You know that when you pay attention you can see worlds within worlds, here and now. You have glimpsed metaphysical realms and you share that with willing others. Your life takes regular unexpected turns and you ever grow and evolve from them.

Out of balance, the **Ethers/Earth** Imprint, early on, told others about their beliefs in other dimensions. You were punished for this and now trust nothing except your own independence and judgment. You know you have a lot of gifts but you have forgotten how to use them. This frustrates you enough that you find it difficult to relax. Something deep inside you is continually prodding you to another plane of existence and it frustrates you.

To Balance Ethers/Earth:

1. Sports. You utilize sports to push yourself beyond limits. Simultaneously, it encourages you to know and take care of your body.

2. Natural health maintenance. Paying attention to nurturing the body grows your appreciation of life. It also reminds you of everything you have in common with all others. Plus, having good health keeps you clear and able to share your deep wisdom bountifully, unconditionally.

3. The Earth. Every way that you can study and appreciate the Earth must be your calling. You intuitively feel the consciousness of the Earth Mother and it gives you joy to honor that.

4. Regular schedules. You flourish with regular schedules or regularly doing tasks you enjoy—like, volunteer work, yoga, gardening.

5. Humanitarianism. You need constant contact with all kinds of people. It grows your perspective and ability to support the evolution of all.

Ethers/Fire

You inherently understand energy. You recognize it as the true universal currency. You continually look for ways to grow it, care for it, and use it abundantly. More than anything, you appreciate enthusiasm and truth.

In balance, the **Ethers/Fire** Imprint masterfully observes and learns from everything. From a young age you developed your own philosophies and were happy to share them with others. At your core you are simple. You want to be happy and to accept all there is.

Out of balance, the **Ethers/Fire** Imprint takes over every situation. You want to be in charge because others are not getting things done correctly and are too slow to figure out how to do things better. You expect everyone to pay full attention to you and to believe you without question. Simultaneously, you demand that everyone around you be enthusiastic, happy and ever improving.

How to Balance Ethers/Fire Imprint:

1. Keep moving. Do as much as you can each day even when you don't immediately feel like it. This grows your energy and automatically reveals where and how to refine your vision.

2. Follow your heart. Truth is utterly essential to you. You must do what you believe in or become "salespersons" (just kidding, but you get the idea).

3. Make your life a work of art. Put creativity into every single thing. Refine constantly and appreciate the beauty of the process.

4. Eat well. If you have a strong metabolism, resist the urge to just eat everything that is put in front of you. Instead, hold out for the foods that comfortably, happily, even out your energy.

5. Share. Generosity lights your fire. Freely give of yourself and your energy to others. If people show willingness to learn, let them see your visions. Show them how the universe works. Offer them the path of abundance.

Ethers/Water

Living with an open heart is not a phrase or an idea. It is a full-on experience with unexpected doorways to healing and new love. That is the core of **Ethers/Water**. You may never speak of it, or if you do, you will use simple words that others will just shout over. You long to connect with others so deeply that no love is left untouched. While you dream of other worlds (as all Ethers Imprints do) you know you are home. You trust that you have and are everything you need.

In balance, this Imprint seeks its own kind. You want family everywhere you go and in everything you do. You possess prodigious energy to care. Because of this you can always find ways to fulfill and be fulfilled.

Out of balance, this Imprint relates to nothing and no one. You focus on yourself and eventually you heal. But in the meantime, you exaggerate every negative emotion and explain away the world by saying it was always a hopeless venture. You hate facing your disappointments and are prone to addictions.

Ways to Balance Ethers/Water:

1. Multi-dimensional awareness. Engage your knowingness, energy and sensitivity by multidimensional practices like rituals, yoga, hypnosis, chanting—in short, any natural means to regularly heighten your consciousness. Not only will this enhance your lifeforce and joy it will steer you clear of addiction.

2. Confidants. Cultivate a few long term friends with whom you can utterly be yourself. Because people will seek out your compassionate ear you will need to make sure that you have time, space and people where nothing is expected of you.

3. A beautiful home. Make your home a castle. Fill it with what you love. Keep changing it. Keep admiring it. It will regenerate you more than most anything else.

4. Get out into the world. You are a natural hermit. However, if you are alone too much you will not satisfy your mission to share love with all. Surprise visit the world periodically.

Ethers/Air

Everything is exciting. Everything is a doorway. Everything connects to everything else. These passions fuel **Ethers/Air**. You want everybody to know about these wonders and you will sometimes bypass food, sleep and patience to let them know. You were born at the right time. You are an information expert during the information Age. From the time you were young, you wanted to learn and share your learnings with everyone. Everyday brings newness and you don't want to miss a single thing.

In balance, people with an **Ethers/Air** Imprint understand why people do what they do. You remain detached from judgment and happily spend your days helping people create the lives of their real choices. Because you have explored everything, you know all the tips, products, and most efficient routes to people fulfilling their desires. Seeing people happy is your great thrill.

When out of balance, you are the only person who knows the right way to do something. You don't waste time making anyone do it your way. And if they don't appreciate their dictatorship, it's THEIR problem. Obviously, they are not intelligent enough to understand you.

How to Balance an Ethers/Air Imprint:

1. Rest/sleep. This Imprint tends to be "on" all the time. It's crucial for you to have complete down time. Wearing an eye mask will deepen your sleep, rest, meditations.

2. Friends. It takes a lot, and a lot of different, people to entertain and satisfy and **Ethers/Air**.

3. Learning. This is your vocation in life, so it is crucial for you to be "in school" for your whole life. A personal library is a must.

4. Dancing. You need movement and body awareness. Combine that with a total passion for freedom and dance is your great ally.

Note: In our years of learning Elemental Birth Imprints we have met only a few humans with Ethers in their Imprints. Overall, there is an otherworldliness to them. It makes them unique yet while they are growing up they can be tremendously challenged by their Imprint. They don't always get how to belong or even why they should. If there are young Ethers Imprints in your family or acquaintance, give them extra kindness. Repeat the rules regularly and patiently. Understand that it may take them longer to integrate everyday reality as they are viewing many dimensions and possibilities simultaneously.

Unusual Elemental Birth Imprints we have known

By far most of you humans were born with an Elemental Birth Imprint that has two different Elementals. They help you to utilize polarities to heal. Obviously we couldn't write about all the unique things that make up your Elemental Birth Imprint for every Elemental Birth Imprint is totally unique. Why? Because it was born in its own perfect time and place and special circumstances. It will be used perfectly and uniquely by its owner/operator.

When there have been different Elemental Birth Imprints, we felt that person's soul had extra things they wanted to learn and heal in this life. This doesn't make their journey easier (usually not) but it always makes things interesting. It adds adventure. It tests courage and it shows the people around them how to deal with challenge.

To give you a sense about how unusual Elemental Birth Imprints can function we offer these examples so that you can feel more and more of what Elemental Birth Imprints are and how you can work with them.

A small minority of people are born with Elemental Birth Imprints not exactly listed in this BOOK. Their souls choose to learn and to evolve as much as they can in this lifetime. So they stack the deck in their favor with an unique Elemental Birth Imprint that attracts and grows adventures—quirks of fate, extra challenges in order to heal. Here are some of the types of unique Imprints we have met:

1. **Elemental Birth Imprints with the two Elements very close together (for instance, 55% /45%).** This is like being ambidextrous. You get to choose your habitual orientation and when you want to change. It is most kind if you choose to do this consciously. That encourages you to manifest your true desires with as many resources as possible. However if you slip back and forth unconsciously between your "dominant" Element and the 2nd Element, you may manifest unwittingly from denial or addiction.

2. **Elemental Birth Imprints with widely spaced %'s (like 90/10).** In balance, this Elemental Birth Imprint wields power and focus readily. They seem to be born knowing what to do (at least in certain circumstances). However, when overly stressed these people try to dominate their circumstances arbitrarily. They find it hard to get along with people (and vice versa); things happen but usually the hard way. While this Elemental Birth Imprint ultimately gains strength from this, the friction is painful. They start to feel like they are the only ones doing what they are doing.

3. **Very specific %'s (like 73/27).** No kidding. We don't know what those numbers mean. Maybe we never will. But the people who have them inherently recognize them. Sometimes they know exactly what those numbers mean. Perhaps the numbers keep showing up and speaking to them during their life. Sometimes it simply marks this incarnation as an unusual or important one. Maybe the birth itself was different. We don't know what each number means, we just know that it translates to a special message for that person. We always invite them to keep listening.

4. **More than two Elementals in the Elemental Birth Imprint.**

While we have never met a five Elemental Imprint we have met people with three or four Elements in their Imprints. We are utterly familiar with two Element Elemental Birth Imprints because we meet so many of them. We don't know exactly what these others mean because of their rarity. It feels like the more Elements in the Birth Imprint, the more it is about relationship. They are an exponential geometry. This brings those persons more gifts and more distractions potentially. Perhaps you with extra Elements in your Birth Imprint will tell us how that unfolds. (We always ask for that feedback.)

When there are three Elements in a person's Birth Imprint it gives them the opportunity to write their own story. Depending on the percentages they can have one or two of the Elementals to focus on to learn intimately and to heal. Or they can have two Elementals to express their main Elemental heart. In geometry and numerology, three's create initial manifestation. They take the polarities of two and add another Element for greater movement and creativity. When you have more than two Elementals in an Imprint sometimes what speaks loudest are the Elements not present in the Elemental Birth Imprint. They become invisible partners complementing what is already familiar.

While we have never met a human with all five Elementals in their Imprint (Maybe they don't need to exist on this dimension?) we have met a few people with three or four Elementals in their Imprint. This translates to people with extra gifts and resources. It means they have energies ready, on-hand, to bridge to other needs, circumstances and possibilities. It is a wonder and a full-time occupation. It calls to mind the expression, " . . .to him that much is given, much is expected." With these inherent energies they will be continually invited to adventure in new realms for the benefit of all.

Two or one Elements in an Imprint focus unceasingly on the most immediate and timely—even relentless—healing. From birth, these people have their shoulder to the grindstone dealing continually with the issues of the day. This is what is most needed and that is why, by far, the majority of humans will be born with one or two Elementals in their Birth Imprints.

None of this means that how many Elements in your Imprint is better or worse. It's not even old versus new. Every single Elemental Birth Imprint lives and breathes as an absolutely essential utterly irreplaceable piece of lifeforce-in-evolution. Everybody is completely needed (Talk about ultimate job security!) and is fully encouraged to join the most magnificent transition between the Ages that the Earth Mother and humans have ever seen together.

Talking about and connecting with your Elemental Birth Imprint simply orients you in life where everything is seamlessly and lovingly in union. Once you are born you seem to forget that origin and you flail about in stormy seas. It is the gift of quantum leap evolution from the Piscean Age to the Aquarian Age that as a species we are remembering . . . we are remembering who we truly are . . . we are remembering freedom, immortality and invisibility (more on this later). We are remembering we are free to choose ourselves . . . we are remembering that we are healing and becoming anew with absolutely generous universal support . . . we are remembering that each of us has been given an Elemental Birth Imprint - a map home. Simply knowing this (even before we act upon it) reorients us in full truth. It shows us our gloriously inescapable roots in unlimited lifeforce. Elemental Birth Imprints cannot truly be judged or understood. They are gifts that we can choose by acting upon them or not. How we act upon these gifts in this fast approaching Aquarian Age is still being written. We are creating the parameters as we go.

People with three Elements in their Elemental Birth Imprint tend to manifest more immediately and more continually. They possess innate momentum. If they are unbalanced, they tend to experience imbalance fully. If they are in balance, they like exploring those circumstances fully. Either way, their speedy and continual efforts call down the thunder and lightning—true Elemental displays.

People with four Elements in their Elemental Birth Imprint come with a ready beingness. While they can do anything, their core needs to flow in the natural cycles of things easily. They can exhibit a grace not easily found. They tend to manifest being taken care of and/or taking care of everything immediately around them.

These people are especially challenged when they fall out of balance. Most all of the other Elemental Birth Imprints innately use the Elemental/s they were not natally imprinted with to "push off of" with force and energy. Because those other Elementals are initially less familiar, they are springboards to different perceptions and therefore new action and learning. Think of those "missing" Elementals like a stranger that you confide in during a crisis. Because there is no immediate attachment between you, you can find real truth unexpectedly. People with four Elements in their Birth Imprints are born familiar with all the physical Elements/Elementals. When familiarity breeds contempt, they find it hard to seek out new wisdom. You can tell by their incessant questions or their dislike of changing their well-worn modus operandi.

5. <u>**Underpinnings and Overlays**</u>

Just when you get a little familiar with all the numeric possibilities of Elemental Birth Imprints, life jumps in with a new adventure. Some people have underpinnings to their Elemental Birth Imprints. For instance, if you are **Air/Water with an underpinning of Fire**, you will play out all the **Air/Water** possibilities, and when you get good and stuck, the **Fire** Elemental will be the next tool in your tool belt. In a crisis then, the **Fire** Elemental is at the ready to ground you to the **Earth** with change, creativity and vision. And if the Fire cannot be immediately accepted, it will frustrate, explode and demand extra attention until healing is integrated.

Underpinnings offer themselves as agents of extra grounding when you need them the most. If abused, they bring on extra stubbornness. As ever, it is a choice.

Overlays imbue you with continual inspiration. Unlike Underpinnings, they do not need a crisis to show up. They whisper the wisdom of your Spirit in the most everyday matters. It could be easy to miss them. Yet, Overlays are quietly determined. Even when they have been routinely disregarded, they grow on you. Their natural gentleness offends nothing, not even your defenses. And so, they slip in like unnoticed seeds in your positive foundation. Bit by bit through the influence of the other Elementals, they grow . . . Until one day, you have a force of magnificent affirmations and role models.

If you listen to your Overlay, it is hard to stay down—you will fall and you will get up repeatedly. Overlays remind you of the bigger picture. They bridge to the Ethers when nothing else seemingly can. When people with Overlays act out of balance, they isolate themselves from the everyday world. They continually focus on other realities, sometimes neglecting their bodies and their obligations. They are like fervent converts who only see one way of being and sometimes run over the other options available in their relentless insistence upon their way of life.

In summary, extra permutations in an Elemental Birth Imprint brings you extra gifts and extra challenges as surely as sunset follows sunrise. If you are born with these extra gifts you are linking yourself to different variations of Elemental cycles. You chose this. Resolve to find the extra blessings in all of it.

If you possess a fairly straight-forward Elemental Birth Imprint, rejoice in your focus and simplicity. Or, as the Dalai Lama says, "the purpose of lives is to be happy." And if you still want more adventure, just align with other Elemental as a continual option. Invite them or don't invite them as you wish. We are free-will beings. Grab a little extra **Fire** and paint yourself a new path. That is what this Age is all about.

6. **<u>Totally Unexpected "Whatevers!"</u>**

Just when we grasped most every Elemental Birth Imprint possibility life grinned and threw us a curve. We understood that once your soul selects your Elemental Birth Imprint it remains constant for your entire incarnation/life. Then we met a person we will call Gena. She was born an Earth/Water. She was also born a German Jew during World War II. Her family was one of the last to make it out of Germany alive (although not all of them), just ahead of their orders to go to a "relocation" camp. It took two years for her parents, her young sister, and herself, to finally immigrate to the United States. During all of that time, Gena's parents insisted that everything was fine; they even made their escape a party. Emotionally, Gena was stretched to the max yet had no ready outlet for all that drama and insecurity. So what did Gena do? She cut off her Water Element. She spent the next fifty-plus years living an **Earth** Elemental Birth Imprint. She never cried, and complaining was out of the realm of possibility. In short, she survived. She coped by focusing on what was happening here and now and working in the ways that were appreciated by the world at large.

Maybe it saved her sanity. It did postpone her healing. When Gena found out that she had cut off her Water Elemental in her Birth Imprint, she chose to grow it back. Now she cries all the time. She actually *feels* her emotions, recognizes what wants to be healed and embraces it. It ain't easy but true healing never is in the short term. It always asks more of us than we immediately have to give. And, that is the good news. Just ask Gena who now is finally what she always dreamed to be: an artist. Growing back the Water Elemental grew back her dreams and the means to manifest them.

It is true that in many years of doing and sharing Elemental Birth Imprints we have only met one Gena—someone who actually altered her chosen Birth Imprint. Yet it only takes once for us to realize that these Imprints manifest both regularly and unexpectedly. Anything is possible. What we learned from Gena was to honestly look at our Elemental Birth Imprints and to learn from them without judgment. When we are freely unconditional we free ourselves from everyday expectation and roles and rules. Maybe gravity does not apply. Maybe you can change your Elemental Birth Imprint and heal in unexpected ways. We love adding this little bit of mystery and magic to the recipe of Elemental Birth Imprints. We trust that it will fuel you in the most intriguing, splendid way you decide. You get to choose.

Homework

Are you really aligning with the Elementals, or are you just reading about them? Either way, our Spirits have whispered to us that the blessing of homework is in order. So please take these tasks to heart so that you can write your own path even as you read this BOOK.

1. Every morning, align with all of the Elementals in this order: **Earth**; **Fire**; **Water**; **Air**; **Ethers**. How do you align? BE each of the Elementals in turn. At the core, breathe like each one. Then feel their different qualities filling your body and your awareness. Imprint this in whatever way occurs to you naturally in the moment. Let go of "trying" or "striving." Be. Be and breathe the Elementals one at a time. And if you didn't get it the first time, do it again. Your life and evolution are at stake. Invest time and energy in this and you will reap "Woows!" a thousand-fold. You can't get better odds than that.

2. All day long BE whatever Elemental invites you to become it. It is best not to over-think this task. Let the spontaneity of the Elementals trump your arbitrary ways and habits. Sit like **Earth**. Dance like **Fire**. Nap like **Water**. Tell the best stories like **Air**. Smile like **Ethers**. Wear an Elemental like a fantastic all-encompassing costume. In the whole time you wear it, sound like that Elemental; snack like it; ground like it; wink like it; let it come and go through your pores until your own personality is a willing passenger instead of the driver of your vehicle. Of course, don't do anything insane, just align until no one has to explain to you what that means.

3. Every night just before bedtime (but hopefully when you are still at least semi-awake) finish your day by aligning with one chosen Elemental. Ask the Elementals, "Which one of you wants to help me release the worries and problems of the day and meet me in the Dreamtime clear and free?" Whichever one raises its hand, accept the invitation (even if you had *hoped* for a different dance partner.). Like the shoe folks say, "Just do it." Surrender your everyday little picture to your chosen Elemental. That way it can show you magic that has never before now been seen by you. When you willingly free your movement with an Elemental, alchemy always answers. Change comes. Lead turns into gold.

Once you have loosened your death grip on your daily fears, your open heart will seamlessly bond with your Elemental. You both will enter the Dreamtime and unveil new consciousness. Relax if you don't understand at all. It just means you are being taught a new language. Yippee! Sounds pretty good any way that you say it.

4. Journal. Have a journal or some recording device at the ready always, especially by your bed. When you wake up with Elementally-flavored dreams, write them down. Speak them into a digital recorder. Not enough time? Just note the date and a few buzz-words. Now you are developing a new habit, a habit of union and aligning. Your journal offers living proof. When your stubborn defenses show up (and be kind, they have kept you alive to this moment) read pertinent passages to them. If that doesn't convince them that you are an evolving Elemental being, read it to them again. Read it louder. Act it out, complete with gestures and costumes. When it comes to habits, repetition rules. After all, you weren't born talking. You had to learn it over and over for years, and even then, you couldn't get the "s's" quite right. You practiced until you were fluent. Same thing here. Practice and record.

New Wisdoms

Elemental Birth Imprints showed up in our consciousness at the exact right moment. Humans are evolving beyond their previous hard-won knowledge. Now we have jumped into the abyss of evolution and are waiting to land in new space.

Whenever we fully let go of what we have known, new wisdom will always present itself, jumping up to find us. And it is always unexpected, currently inexplicable and precisely timely. Lucky for us.

Elemental Birth Imprints is one of those new wisdoms. Its arrival proves we are ready for it even before we believe that. When we listen to the language of this new wisdom's qualities, it reflects back to us all that we really are and what we are becoming.

For example, Elemental Birth Imprints go to the core of lifeforce and matter. They are simply therefore all-encompassing. Their impact lands surely and can last a lifetime. They are non-judgmental, hence they come ready-made to accept us and to be used efficiently with any other loving philosophies and growth.

Elemental Birth Imprints can be used anywhere anytime. They tell our stories without need for justification. They support our healing in more ways than we can count. At the core they speak a single word: UNION.

Humans are brave souls who embody Spirits in a dimension where they choose to initially forget the divinity that powered them there in the first place. How? Humans do this by experiencing an often traumatic and potent birthing that seems to tear them apart from their mother, from complete nurturance, and ultimately, from Spirit. Why? Humans do this because remembering and being divine are inevitable. Even as we read this BOOK on a Sunday under a cozy blanket, we are divine immortals. When you are late picking up your kids from school, you are still audacious pioneers. When we pick up the dog poop in the yard, we are still magnificent Elemental beings getting to know every facet of life. Underneath it all, we are so unconditional that we even accept forgetting - the all pervasive illusion of separation—in short, we incarnate through separation so that we can offer Spirit and unconditional love to everything, even that seeming break from Spirit. We are ready and we are remembering. Elemental Birth Imprints know this. They sprung themselves on us when our willingness was high and our need for support was great. They show us that we are union, we are a part of everything and everything is a part of us. Going through separation makes the re-union sweeter.

So now we are integrating Elemental Birth Imprints as quickly as possible. They help us to heal when we don't have words and ways. They show us how to act upon the union that we already are. They are tools of the greatest evolution humans have ever attempted.

While healing happens between ourselves and our own souls, it does not stay a private matter. Elemental Birth Imprints are our pathway to union with ourselves and by definition with others.

Because Elemental Birth Imprints are new their uses are still being developed. The vision that comes to us is around a school. Since this method is new, it matches new humans vibrationally and readily. Picture this: Young school kids sharing their Elemental Birth Imprints all day long. They play them and practice them with each other. Once they are easily familiar with them, they take them home and teach them to their families. Then there would be immediate, continually reinforcing environments to use Elemental Birth Imprints to their shining best.

Children are closer to union typically than adults. They are more likely to remember their wholeness even when they cannot name it by anyone else's standards. When we become childlike again we automatically go to the core; we automatically align with the Elementals; we easily take on our Elemental Birth Imprints and wear them out into the world. What a magnificent evolution that is!

We dedicate the next few pages to early Elemental Birth Imprints - Elemental Birth Imprints as they happen spontaneously and child-like. Early Elemental Birth Imprints show how people manifest these Imprints when they are very young and close to union (and Elemental Birth Imprints are union). Ages zero to four would be the average ages we are relating to with this. When you absorb these entries, look for your children in them (or the child in you) and learn from them. Find the inner-child-you that wants to work, play and evolve on the outside as well. The following Birth Imprints are like the ones previously described except these emphasize child-like manifestation.

Early Earth Elemental Birth Imprint

These kids are immediately curious about their bodies. While they may not be the first ones to roll over or walk, they like to observe and learn about everything. They are patient. They are willing to wait for things to come in their own time because every moment is full of activity and adventure when you are paying attention.

Early Earth/Earth Elemental Birth Imprint

These children like structure. They want to climb on it to see what will bend it, break it, or make it strong. Once they know, they want to build on it. While they don't always like boundaries, oftentimes they offer them a space they can completely fill with their own energy and ideas.

Early Earth/Fire Elemental Birth Imprint

Once they get the hang of the body, they love jumping, running, rolling, as much and as fast as they can. They like putting enthusiasm into everything. Many of them are natural inventors. While they don't like restriction, they appreciate having a say in the rules that apply to them.

Early Earth/Water Elemental Birth Imprint

These kids prize quiet above loud. Calm above chaotic. They hone in on mom, family and dependable people and patterns. These kids are quietly absorbing the rules of life and imprinting them upon themselves indelibly.

Early Earth/Air Elemental Birth Imprint

They so want to talk. They yearn to be understood. The world is a Legos Superstation that they want to build in their own image. That's why they can't get too many ideas.

Early Earth/Ethers Elemental Birth Imprint

These kids take in everything deeply. They remain calm under most situations and manage to communicate telepathically easily. If you tune into them they will utilize their bodies and the immediate environment to make themselves clearly understood.

Early Fire Elemental Birth Imprint

They want everything RIGHT AWAY. They are not daunted by noise and activity. They simply want to get into the fracas themselves. From the first moment they are testing their wills. They need to know how they can attract whatever they want in their world. Do your best to repeat the rules patiently and firmly. This encourages creativity instead of stubbornness.

Early Fire/Fire Elemental Birth Imprint

Wow. Many of them hit the pavement running. They want to walk now. They want to drive now. They want to be in charge now. Give them many varied and ever-changing outlets to engage their desires and quickness. Repetition can irritate them even when needed. Also, many of them come with a strong metabolism and digestive tract. They crave fuel in every way.

Early Fire/Earth Elemental Birth Imprint

Look at how bright-eyed they are! From the first breath they engage you. They laugh. They make faces. They love attention. If they get regular touch they will learn so quickly about everything that their parents will need to take notes to keep up with them.

Early Fire/Water Elemental Birth Imprint

They crave security yet are bored by routine. They want the world to entertain them. And when it does, they give it their heart. They bond with their loved ones tremendously and in their presence like to experiment and risk new adventures.

Early Fire/Air Elemental Birth Imprint

Look out! These are the screamers! They want to develop their lungs and their voices early. Talk to them from the first second. To be included in everything excites and calms them at the same time. If you pay attention you will see that they are learning early to communicate. Follow their lead and everybody will learn new things.

Early Fire/Ethers Elemental Birth Imprint

They are dramatic beings. They know they are here for great purpose and can't wait to get started. Give them as much independence as possible. Multiple sensory stimuli feed them body and soul. Make sure that they are introduced to as many different beings as they will allow as often as possible. Sometimes these young humans will start remembering in their dreams. As soon as they can talk, ask, "What did you dream of last night?"

Early Water Elemental Birth Imprint

They look content don't they? They are still living in the world as if they were in utero. They do not immediately break the bonds of dependency, telepathy and empathy with their parents. They watch you for signs of how to BE. When they feel secure they will find friends everywhere. When they are insecure, they will fuss or disengage from the world.

Early Water/Water Elemental Birth Imprint

Intense. Expressive. Mimicking. They like to listen. Give them a rich and varied sound environment. It will open their hearts and steady their nerves. Some of them will require familiar faces around them constantly for a few years. While this seems like a huge investment in time and energy, it is exactly that: an investment. It encourages and develops deep trust and self esteem.

Early Water/Earth Elemental Birth Imprint

Everything fascinates them. They are extremely tactile, and massage, from the start of their life, grounds them. It helps them to be more daring when need be.

Early Water/Fire Elemental Birth Imprint

Moody. Changeable. Inquisitive. Bright. Easily frustrated. These young humans want to grow up immediately. They like being in charge of anything possible as soon as possible. Find ways for them to be self-determining. Rich with imagination, they need creative outlets. Finger-painting is superb.

Early Water/Air Elemental Birth Imprint

They want to talk to you. They want to ask how your day is going. Actually they want to ask every question possible. They love to be engaged in every facet of family life.

Early Water/Ethers Elemental Birth Imprint

These babies crave comfort and closeness. Sometimes they don't seem too sure about having left the womb. They are learning at quiet, profound all-encompassing levels. Actively communicate telepathically with them. Work with them energetically.

Early Air Elemental Birth Imprint

These young beings are fun. They like focusing on the people around them. As soon as they can, they will engage and charm you. Their moods are quick and usually happy.

Early Air/Air Elemental Birth Imprint

They notice changes in their environment and love to be entertained by them. Infinitely curious, they will try to walk and talk as soon as possible. Sometimes their nervous systems get overloaded. When this happens, low peaceful music brings them back into their bodies.

Early Air/Earth Elemental Birth Imprint

Even from the start they are logical. Show them how things work, especially machines and toys. When they have enough activities nothing bothers them. Boredom is their worst enemy.

Early Air/Fire Elemental Birth Imprint

They love to have fun. They enjoy colors and lights. They prefer being stimulated to being calm and will grow rapidly.

Early Air/Water Elemental Birth Imprint

While it might not show, they are watching everything. They are learning everything. And they easily remember what they have learned. They crave a home where everyone is getting along and like to hear laughter and conversation.

Early Air/Ethers Elemental Birth Imprint

They spend a lot of time multidimensionally. Some time travel. What they do will not always fit in assumed context. Learn from them as much as you can. They will teach you what they remember as soon as possible.

Early Ethers Elemental Birth Imprint

They focus on their parents. They look for every way to bond with them and to make them happy. When their mothers are pleased, all is right with the world. While they possess immediate wisdom, they do not always demonstrate co-ordination and balance. While learning how to use their bodies they may need extra support.

Early Ethers/Ethers Elemental Birth Imprint

Definitely they have an other-world glow. Most of them radiate bright innocence and great willingness to be present. Communicate with them in every way that you can. They understand and can build upon that in their own ways. Most of them are very unique. Do not expect them to fulfill normal timetables and needs.

Early Ethers/Earth Elemental Birth Imprint

They work hard. They put effort into everything. They want to find every way to please you, so much so, that when things don't work out they are disappointed. Fortunately, simple treats are heavenly to them.

Early Ethers/Fire Elemental Birth Imprint

Most things don't happen fast enough for them but when they do, they learn just as quickly. They want to be in charge though they are perfectly willing to share the power with other kind, happy souls.

Early Ethers/Water Elemental Birth Imprint

Calm and peace encourage them. Early on they may sleep more than most. Rest and regeneration will be crucial to them throughout life. When they have enough energy, they will be anything to please you.

Early Ethers/Air Elemental Birth Imprint

They are gifted. Often, they are early talkers and teachers. Whatever they know they are willing to share. As soon as is possible let them meet as many people as possible and they will learn to make friends with anybody all life long.

Recognize yourself? Feel very free in encouraging your innate gifts. Following that path (no matter what your defenses say) only creates more prosperity and blessings. Don't believe it? Absolutely, don't. Go out and find out for yourself. Invest fully in the most spectacular YOU. Try that on and prove whatever reality you choose to, and for, yourself.

Didn't recognize yourself? Unfortunately this is understandable. Most of us—actually all of us—changed almost immeasurably from how we were born to how we are at this moment. Fortunately, now you can embark on the path of immeasurable healing. If you really can't see how beautifully you started life, go to the source. Get quiet. Open your heart. This moment is just for you and nothing else. Ask your little child self, "What are we really like?" Wait for the answer. It will come if you persevere. It's possible that at first you'll pick up a lot of static on this channel between the two of you. Defenses and doubts often obscure the truth . . . but only temporarily. Keep asking until you know your own truth. Act upon it. You will see how incredibly wonderful that is.

Plan B:

If you need extra support finding your truth, speak with children. They are closer to remembering. They are not so far away from just being and living their Elemental Birth Imprint every day. Follow their lead. Ask their advice. As our Spiritual Grandmother says, "You will heal. This much is inevitable."

Compassion

Elemental Birth Imprints are new. Try not to squash them right out of the gate. Get to know them gently. Whenever you sidle up to something new you will be excited and scared. The brave human adventurer-you will be thrilled. Even if you don't believe it, you can't help anticipating what is next. That's what you came to this planet to live and breathe.

You will be scared too. Your defenses instinctively sound the alarm whenever something new enters your space. It's called survival. And a lot of times it works pretty well, so be grateful.

Whenever emotions—especially conflicting ones—rise up swiftly, they put a charge on that situation. All that electrical energy is rightfully placed there so that you can be at the ready to act as swiftly as need or desire or crisis requires. Getting back to getting familiar with your Elemental Birth Imprint, you may have to outlast the charge around their newness. Quick conflicting emotions might not give you the clearest picture of your potential relationship with your Elemental Birth Imprint. Yet it is worth the wait. The Imprint has been with you longer than even your birthday. It joined you even before you had a personality that could tell you how you felt about Elemental Birth Imprints. It embodies that Zen koan, "What did your face look like before you were born?"

We know you understand. You've already been told not to judge a book by its cover. Yet, there is another, freer aspect to that. Elemental Birth Imprints live beyond judgment, even beyond understanding. They just are. In trying to work with them, in trying to reunite with them, anything is truly possible in the most positive way not yet imagined.

Consider this: Your Elemental Birth Imprint is completely unique to you. If you trust that then you can work with it in your own most unique way. You make up the rules. You prove it as you wish; nobody else has a say in it.

Really integrate all of this. If you are reading with just your mind-alone you are missing an adventure. Take a moment now and join us in aligning with the Elementals so that you and every new wonder you have found here comes home to roost.

*Breathe with the **Earth** Elemental. Breathe like you are the **Earth** Elemental. How about that. Golden prana is filling up your every cell slowly and luxuriously. You have all the time and space in the world. You are all the time and space in the world. Ask, "Which part of my body wants the most attention from the **Earth** Elemental?" Send it that prana. Just sit with it. It might sting. Healing often does. Just stay with it until it's soothed and hushed. Peace fills you and you sigh. Now that you are comfortable in your own skin, it's easier to feel that way about everything else. Give thanks to Momma **Earth** for holding you in Her arms and always welcoming you even when you didn't know it. Say to every part of your body, "I am happy to be here."*

*Breathe **Fire**. This is a fun one. Be a Dragon! Don't you feel invincible? Impossible? And magnificent? Now you are breathing and being **Fire**. Sheer lifeforce is lighting you up. Watch the colors dance around you and swirl in and out with you. What's your favorite color? Dragonfire breathe on it! Now it's all you can see in all directions. The immense gorgeousness of it woows you. Reach out with your breath and sculpt it into something that just gives off joy. Make roses or mountains or seashells, any colors, all colors—you are the painter in charge. This is your inexplicable illogical world and it changes with every whim. Breathe it to your own delight.*

*Breathe **Water**. As you do, remember this is how you started out on this planet. You were submerged in it. It was your devoted partner in everything. Smile at that memory. Appreciate the family of it. Most of you is still water. When you appreciate your memories and truths the rivers inside of you smile back. Most of you turns happy instantly. Breathe that a little deeper. Breathe that right on through resistance and hurt that havn't found their way yet. Immerse yourself in the clear fluidity of **Water**. There is nothing and no one to impress. Be yourself and just decide that is ok no matter what. Here. Now. Happiness is a choice. You can't get it wrong. You can't get it right.*

*Breathe **Air**. Kind of redundant . . . until you consider that a lot of the time you are not actually breathing. Many times you are holding your breath so you don't have to feel pain. You're projecting that you will be afraid. So you keep away from breathing and life. Sometimes you are quietly gasping for **Air** and you don't even know it. It's a habit. You've repeated half-breathing so long that it almost seems like the real thing. So fill up. Surrender to the **Air**. Drink it in. Focus on it completely. Do this and do this until you get to know it again. Make "How I love **Air**" your new project. Give it as much time and energy as you can muster every day. Starting now.*

*Breathe **Ethers**. There is no way on Earth to do it. Imagination and Spirit must launch you. Ask for them. Ask for them to take you where your guides and totems live, where everybody knows you at the core, with nothing to hide and everything to share. Where are you? Who are you? Breathe an answer. Let the **Ethers** keep shaping you. You can have any dream. It has always been this way. You are just taking the time to notice it now, to trust it into reality. Take it a step further: Affirm out loud, "I can be any dream." How do you breathe the **Ethers**? Let them breathe you.*

Additions . . .

Aligning with the Elementals and integrating your Elemental Birth Imprint are more than enough for a lifetime. But what about an Age? We are shifting from one Age to another. We are evolving. Elemental Birth Imprints have come into our consciousness so that we can share them with each other and support our evolution together. To do this we are going to explore how each Elemental might dance with all of the Elemental Birth Imprints we have shared here. When you know that, you know how to consciously balance yourself at the core and you know how you can choose to interact with every other energy, therefore, every other person, place, time or possibility. So here we will go through what might happen when you add any of the Elementals to all of the Elemental Birth Imprints we have been working with in this BOOK. Adding an Elemental can mean breathing with it or aligning with it consciously to balance your Elemental Birth Imprint according to what circumstances life presents you. Or it can show you how you might interact with other people whose Elemental Birth Imprints contain those Elementals. While we experience healing as an individual journey, how we interact (our Elemental Birth Imprints) with other people (their Elemental Birth Imprints) and the continually moving dance of the Elementals upon the Earth reflects back to us clarity and possibilities we may not find otherwise. So as we list how the different Elementals combine with individual Elemental Birth Imprints you get the opportunity to feel the dance of these Elementals within you. Focus on that opportunity to learn and grow.

Adding Earth to the following Elemental Birth Imprints:

Earth– Familiarity and comfort reign in this combination. Adding **Earth** to **Earth** reminds you of the endless perfect changing seasons. When you are hurt and confused, adding the **Earth** through friends and walking in nature brings you back to your body and empowers you. It reminds you that you can respond to anything, and you do. You always do.

RED FLAG: The caveat here is stubbornness. If you get too entrenched in the **Earth** Elemental you lose perspective. It is possible to ground so much that you never move even when you need to do so. When you refuse to yield to the natural flow of life, everything gets harder. You are so brittle you break. You throw out your back, you fall down, but no worries, ultimately, inevitably, you are learning. You will get stronger as you cultivate surrender to fluidity. Yoga is calling out to you.

Earth/Earth– Same as the above, with greater emphasis and energy.

RED FLAG: Stodgy. Gloomy. Focused on morality for morality's sake alone. Has anybody called you any of these things? Quick; write down what you were feeling and what you were doing because of this. These are priceless clues to how/when/why you go out of balance. And you didn't even know you were out of balance. You assumed that you <u>must</u> be right. Always. All ways. Perseverance under stress is your middle name. Use it. When you are out of balance, change your mind. Do something else. Do something new. Just about anything different will shake up your array of negative habits.

Earth/Fire– On a good day, adding **Earth** gives more time and space to the sometimes endless stream of creativity here. It calms things down when **Fire** is raging out of control. It integrates passion and incredible possibilities into immediately usable parameters.

RED FLAG: Watch out so that the inherent limits of **Earth** don't squash **Fire**. Its creativity just needs to dance, that's how it produces wonder even though it will go through silly and impossible on the way. If authority figures (**Earth** Elemental) beat you over the head with the rules you might start believing that the **Fire's** spontaneity is wrong, and then, it goes away and there are less silly wonders to admire.

Earth/Water– The natural symbiosis of this Elemental Birth Imprint usually rolls gracefully with more **Earth–** You put your compassion to work. Overall, you produce more of what you love.

RED FLAG: Watch out for extra judgments. This much **Earth** sometimes takes over and decides arbitrarily what is right and wrong without allowing for unconditional love and acceptance. (Hint: Add more **Water**.)

Earth/Air– The easily defined meets the indefinable. This Elemental Birth Imprint loves **Earth** when it needs to find ways to share its wonder and fresh ideas with everyone. Secretly, you are grateful for the extra organization and clarity that comes in with the **Earth** Elemental. Sometimes **Air** is all talk. Sometimes **Earth** is all action. Putting them together invents practical new support/tools/systems for all.

Red flag: Too much **Earth** overpowers the whimsy of **Air**. Instead of cuddling it into encouragement, it regulates it to death and the **Air** just blows away. It figures that none of those new ideas had a chance to happen anyway.

Earth/Ethers–
This is a match made on heaven and earth. **Ethers**, especially in young people, is a lot of energy and potential to ground. It discombobulates most people, at least initially. Bring in extra **Earth** and **Earth/Ethers** finds a home. You feel safe enough to belong and to share.

Red flag: There is not a lot to be wary of here. The **Ethers** can handle just as much **Earth** as is freely offered. However, on a dark day, too much **Earth** sounds jaded, skeptical. It is afraid to reach to the sky for what it truly craves.

Fire–
What happens when you put a log on a good fire? The fire now has dependable sustaining fuel to show off its beauty and to warm your toes. The **Earth** gets to transform some of its matter quickly and easily. Everybody benefits.

Red flag: Too much **Earth** puts out the **Fire**. It is that simple. Its need to define kills off the inherent spontaneity and transformation of **Fire**.

Fire/Fire–
All that **Fire** is always looking for **Earth** to fuel it. It is happy. In the right circumstances it is brilliantly co-creative. In the vast changes that follow this meeting, magic must happen.

Red flag: Feeding the **Fire** too much is reckless literally. You get overly optimistic without practicality. Accidents can happen. When it is too big, **Fire** is a bully.

Fire/Earth–
There is a changing, grounded flow here. You have the ability to switch from the big picture to the details. Really, there is nothing you can't do. You have the key to every great inventor, builder, leader: perseverance.

Red flag: Bossy! Combining these Elements is so unstoppable they can get power-mad. Don't let this happen to you. If you start feeling, "It's my way or the highway," go climbing barefoot. Touch the patience and the endurance of the **Earth** and then write your perspective.

Fire/Water–
Now you are cooking. Literally. Get it? Sounds like yummy vegetable stew to us. Seriously, how do Elementals come together in nature and tell us everything we need to know about loving, appreciating and working with our own Elemental Birth Imprints? There is no way to say this too much: Adding **Earth** to **Fire/Water** offers security, patience and stamina. **Fire/Water** is then all healing. It loves a little gravity so that it knows it has been taken seriously. The extra validation invites a flourish of creativity and compassion.

Red flag: There is a certain fixedness to this combination. Look for any flexibility in dramatic circumstances. Watch out for stubbornness.

Fire/Air–
Adding **Earth** here is like a well-needed reality check for an adventurous pilot. It offers balance, reason and an awareness of others that show a REAL awareness of them instead of looking at situations as theories only. Perhaps best of all the **Earth** slows you down so that you kindly remember to take care of yourself and to honor your healthy body.

Red flag: Practically speaking there is almost never any danger to watch out for here in adding the **Earth**. The only thing you might feel is stubbornness when you must change.

Fire/Ethers—
Here is where the next wave of technology, magic and spirituality meets the everyday world. What a glorious thing to ground. It gives patience and perspective to unbelievable creativity and possibilities. Together, these three Elements study what was impossible before and make brand new possibilities here and now. You can shake up any deeply held belief and transform it if needed.

Red flag: Proselytizing and not consulting others when needed. Knowing what is best for someone else and not even realizing that you are operating out of that disrespect. Absolute power corrupts absolutely.

Water—
These two Elements together are old-time lovers. They instinctively know how to nurture the other and they automatically do so. **Earth** gives form to the free flow of **Water**. You feel at home.

Red flag: Do you <u>always</u> know what is best? Keep listening. Keep feeling everything so that you can change when needed, constantly. If you find yourself always reacting from the same habits, you are out of balance. Start over. Go to the lake or the beach and ask the **Water** Elemental what to do.

Water/Water—
Adding **Earth** balances excessive emotions. It helps deal with obsessions and gives away old hurts. It comforts and it lets you know that you have been listened to fully. Regeneration follows.

Red flag: Most of the time this is a very positive combination. One of the few down sides is isolation—being too much of a hermit.

Water/Earth—
Here is a big beautiful garden. **Earth** loves to add timeless but regular cycles to everything. **Water/Earth** needs this so that it can nurture the dryness of everyday routines. This is like putting a smile out where it is most needed and yet unexpected. One day, there will be a nice surprise for anybody who wants it.

Red flag: Too sensible; too logical. It calls the emotion unnecessary. Self esteem is utterly undermined and you don't even know it.

Water/Fire—
This is pure intimacy out in the world, freely offered in ways that honor all. **Water/Fire** craves a space to BE. **Earth** gives it a home so that all those feelings are safe enough to be kindly and generously expressed and shared. Everyone benefits.

Red flag: Together these Elements are passion enough to do everything. If there is not perspective you end up helping people who never asked to be helped. You run over their processes with "the best intentions" leading others to ask, "Did anybody get the license plate number of that truck?"

Water/Air—
You **Water/Air** Imprints like uniting opposites. You revel in compassionately joining and feeling all the different parts of you. Adding **Earth** brings comfort. It cares for the body while you focus more energy on the mind, the heart and the soul. Generally speaking, regular balancing with the **Earth** Elemental is exactly what you need and must have all the time.

Red flag: When you are out of balance you believe your heart is leading the way when in fact your defenses and unsatisfied needs rule. Adding **Earth** in this situation helps you to feel justified in your imbalances. You feel like you are in charge and you should be because no one else sees the dangers that you can.

Water/Ethers–
Such sweetness. Healing will always flower in this joining. When our souls asked to come to the **Earth**, this is what we feel like—compassionate, open hearts available to all in a moment's notice as needed.

Red flag: Sometimes you stay away from people because you feel their pain more than they do. Adding **Earth** (out of balance) justifies acting/manifesting from those fears.

Air–
Yes. Nothing brings body and soul together faster than intentional breath. Bringing **Earth** to **Air** makes prana. The result can be happily detached awareness.

Red flag: Conflict. Picture stubbornly unrealistic meeting the real world. They don't integrate smoothly. Or, when they do see eye to eye, they embody, "a little knowledge is a dangerous thing."

Air/Air–
This is like an incredibly happy, energetic two-year old being given access to the worlds best stocked and safest playground. All out fun is inevitable. If this is you (your Imprint), you now have the means to understand and integrate the many, many different views. Now they all have a voice and are satisfied. You will be able to generously share your wisdom and good humor. Parties abound!

Red flag: Can you feel it? This is too dry. Your heart may be MIA because your mind and your mouth are going a mile-a-minute. Your feelings aren't there to listen.

Air/Earth–
You can organize anything, even yourself. You honor time. Efficiency is the gift that you generally and generously bestow upon all. Your lifeforce is important to you therefore you are interested in everything and everybody and you show it.

Red flag: Don't be a know-it-all. You run the danger of taking a few facts and believing that you understand the whole story. Be quiet. Listen to others in turn, even if you think you know better. There is always time and opportunity to learn. Grab it.

Air/Fire–
What a god-send! Sometimes you have all the passion but no timing and no grace. Enter **Earth**. Enter timing, grace and enough motivation to persevere. Dreams will come true, of that you can be sure. This is real-time fun. Everybody else is blissfully involved too.

Red flag: You have boundless energy . . . to do good or bad. When you don't take the time to consider everybody, you are likely to run over people and their feelings. Your most likely targets? Your family and loved ones.

Air/Water— **Earth** brings objectivity and subjectivity as needed when needed. You **Air/Water** people sometimes go to extremes. **Earth** is the great beneficent balancer. Adding this calms your blood pressure, soothes your nerves, and reminds you of that body that forgot you had. An added bonus: When you ground (read add **Earth** Elemental) your family and friends will understand you and you will be rightfully listened to for your real-world inspirations and hunches.

Red flag: You don't know how to focus and you don't know how to objectively prioritize, yet you act on those half-formed ideas. Silly you. Start over. You are probably not grounding enough. Let go of thinking. Go barefoot at the same time. It will all come together, you just don't know how yet. Try to relax while you are waiting.

Air/Ethers— Praise, praise for the **Earth** Elemental and take a double serving! You are inspiration in body—when you remember the in-body part. Everybody wants to rejoice in your creativity. **Earth** translates your otherworldly perspective here and now. Everyone will benefit. Everyone. Your ideas will keep flourishing; the crazy ones will die and give birth to better ones; and you will adore connecting everyone in a vast network of learning and empowered healing.

Red flag: Crazy as it sounds, you might not be reaching high enough with your aspirations. Your down side believes in doubt religiously. Give it up. When all you hear in your head is, "No. No. No. No. No," start over. Start your day and your projects with everything you believe in. Just work on the things that you can say, "Yes," to and grow up to the heights where you are as free as you truly crave.

Ethers— Adding **Earth** to **Ethers** may be the best suited combination for humans to experience. **Ethers** grounded by **Earth** is the definition of human itself. Here is where you find out why you are here. Better yet, now you can act upon it. All is well.

Red flag: When the **Earth** out of balance dominates the **Ethers**, either you are hopelessly dejected or you dominate everyone considering nothing but yourself. Not a pretty picture. Use the Earth Mother as a role model. She is both in charge and a generous servant. She honors Herself and you and shares unstintingly.

Ethers/Ethers— Welcome in genius. You are an old soul looking for compassionate means to translate your awareness to others. Yet you must do this honorably. Everyone is a free-will being. You cannot disrupt their path in any way. Respectfully adding the **Earth** Elemental may be both the most immediate and long-term way to heal yourself while unobtrusively supporting others. You are a natural role model.

Red flag: Same caveats as for the Ethers above, but with this addition: You just don't translate in the real world. You have too much energy and presence to comfortably bridge to others. Likely you need a double dose of Earth Elemental.

Ethers/Earth— There is something very angelic about you. And it is real. While not everyone will understand your innocence coupled with awareness, they will admire it. They will learn from it. You will learn from everyone else. You are true compassion embodied.

Red flag: Doubt. Doubting constantly leads to despair. Despair leads to doing nothing. Even if you don't yet believe it is possible, act upon even the smallest ray of hope. So it quietly. Build upon it. Inevitably you will grow strong and empowered.

Ethers/Fire– Think of Einstein. That is what these three Elementals add up to: Weirdness in a wonderful way. You never look at the same situation in the same way twice and that is a brave and bountiful gift. When you are grounded you are a prolific inventor. Instead of building just in other dimensions, you are bringing it home. Thanks from all the rest of us.

> R*ed flag:* Sometimes you move along at your own pace and this is fine. Other times, it doesn't work. Your careless superiority closes off your awareness and compassion. Everyone gets burnt. No worries. You have the perseverance to apologize and do it differently, and probably, quickly.

Ethers/Water– Some people think you are a saint. There is nothing too difficult or too small for your very kind attention. You love to love. Picture the Dalai Lama beaming away just at you. This is how the rest of us feel in your presence/presents.

> R*ed flag:* Nobody's feelings get hurt like yours. Anything can be misconstrued as having ill intent for you and when you do take it personally, you lose all objectivity. You don't even realize that you could go to the person and try to find out the truth and some harmony. You are closed off. The good news is that innately you still have perspective. Use your tenacity to focus on why you are hurt. Track it down to whatever unresolved hurt is festering in you right now, and therefore, attracting other slights. Focus. Heal yourself. Love yourself.

Ethers/Air– When you look up "unique" in the dictionary there is a picture of you. You embody freedom, individuality and choice in everything you do. While the rest of us don't understand you immediately, you entertain us constantly. You get us giggling about life's weirdness until, hurrah, we get it! We understand too.

> R*ed flag:* You are too weird for words and you just keep using more and more of them. And sometimes they are too big for even Google to understand. Slow down. After you say something, rest, breathe, listen. Come up with a fail-safe ritual that will bring you back into your body after Scotty beamed you up.

SUMMARY: When you add an Elemental to your life you are putting its qualities into motion and manifestation. Manifestation is the quickest byword for **Earth** Elemental. When you add it to your Birth Imprint or it is added from the outside in relationship/circumstance, you give yourself the immediate opportunity to be in body or not. If you ground into yourself and the Earth, you gain empowerment, choices, patience and stamina. In short, you become a mini-model of the Earth Mother Herself. If you don't know what that means, go to the woods or the river or some unspoiled nature and watch, listen, and ask the Earth Mother to show you Her true essence. You will want to be in body to receive this.

When you cannot integrate the **Earth** Elemental (or can't get all the way into your body) you will probably keep going. But what will be in charge of your decisions and your actions? Likely it will be your "default" settings. These are rote defensive behaviors that we learned to protect ourselves when we were too afraid to really face things and take care of them. When your defenses are running the show, you give yourself very limited, stiff, arbitrary options. You sound like an authority even when you have no idea what is really going on. Secretly, you are a lost child in a world where everything (especially the Earth) is fighting you. Battling with the **Earth** Element invites you to add, "Be here now."

Here is what happens by adding Fire to the following Elemental Birth Imprints:

Earth– Adding **Fire** gets the **Earth** moving until it dances. **Earth** Imprints pretend (even to themselves) that nothing is better than standing extremely still and growing your roots to the center of the **Earth**. While that is pretty splendid, the Earth Mother doesn't stand still and She is the role model here. At Her core, She fumes with explosions and molten lava. She heats us from the inside out. **Fire** to **Earth** brings smiles and constant newness.

Red flag: Impatience with an attitude. Sound familiar? Learn to breathe even in anger (maybe especially then) and you will direct that energy to be grounded. Now it is safer for all.

Earth/Earth– You need this alchemy. Change is constant yet somehow you sometimes manage to forget that. Thankfully you are being reminded. Now you can use muscles you didn't know you had. Your heart opens up like the Sun at noon.

Red flag: Usually it's a case of too little too late. You change but only after you have been offended. The Fire becomes righteous indignation. Run around the block. Get your blood pumping. You have everything you need to do anything wonderful.

Earth/Fire– You have great instincts. Use them. Sometimes a respectful risk is your best move. If you haven't done that recently, go for it. Dream and act big.

Red flag: Too fast. Too slow. You have lost your timing. It is ok. You are just in the middle of a quantum leap evolution. Change has got you by the tail and is spinning you around. Don't take it personally. Always focus on change as your agent of enlightenment and evolution. Give true thanks.

Earth/Water– This is exciting. Definitely things are happening and will keep happening. Feel your way. Keep refining every act until you are aligned with the biggest, bravest most loving picture possible.

Red flag: You act before you speak. In a crisis that may be the very best choice. But if you are doing this constantly in every situation, you are not connecting to all the people around you respectfully. They need to be informed and you need to be clear with your passions. Breathe. Then act.

Earth/Air— You are a crazy one. And you look good while you are doing it. Be bold. Innovation is your strong suit. Show others what you are talking about and you can galvanize a whole community. Ever thought of politics?

Red flag: Mostly you do really well with the addition of **Fire**. Generally, the missing variable is greater intimacy. Risk more than a few words. You are being asked—urged - to open your heart. Do it now before you can stop yourself.

Earth/Ethers– You lead in the most magnificent ways. When inspired, you lead by the light of your own soul. You fearlessly risk. You honor all of lifeforce. You change as invited and you ground it with the determination born of hard-won wisdom.

> *Red flag:* When we are leading, it starts from an instinct to initiate ourselves in new circumstances. This is so honoring there are not words that adequately describe it. Yet, these initiations bring up so many fears that sometimes we try to overpower them. In that struggle, we run over everybody and everything else in the way. We are blinded by fear. However, the true leadership instilled in all of us can always see situations for what they are even after the fact. Apologize. Start over. Let your heart lead instead of fear.

Fire– Yep! Some of you are squealing in delight and others of you are screaming in terror, "Add **Fire** to **Fire**, are you nuts!" Absolutely. Yet it would be unconscionable to not live life to its fullest. It demands that of us and we respond in kind. We are welcoming possibilities that never expressed before now.

> *Red flag:* Yes. Something is going to get burnt. You will grieve. You will struggle. Just accept all of it. All different forms of change are inevitable. Whatever gets burned away will resurrect Phoenix-like after you graciously surrender to change.

Fire/Fire– You can learn and understand anything by instinct. Why? Because you are relentlessly truthful. If anything rings false to you, you do whatever it takes to get to the truth at the core. That's where you align. That's where we will find you—always ready to give birth to greatness.

> *Red flag:* Don't forget to bring your body. You can be utterly reckless. Accident prone doesn't begin to cover it. Wiggle your toes before you act. Touch your heart before you speak. Immediate gratification at all costs is dangerous.

Fire/Earth– With **Fire** added we have excitement, dynamic, well-planned explosions! You probably get all the attention - deservedly so. You inspire us beyond the pinnacle of dreams. You lead us into the unknown still holding our hands and smiling, "It's going to be more than ok." Doubtless, we are afraid. The unknown has not always been our favorite ally; but you know better. When we go there together ultimately our excitement trumps our fears. Our species is evolving.

> *Red flag:* You just need a sprinkling of patience. We can smell it. But while you are still brewing it, you needlessly hurt the feelings of those around you. And it is silly because they were following you whole-heartedly, doing their absolute best. Remember that. "We are all doing our best." Calm down.

Fire/Water– Shamanic. You easily move between the worlds wherever they are. Your courage brings back unimaginable wisdom to your tribe. You are a visionary that lovingly tells your family and community what dangers to avoid.

> *Red flag:* Regularly walk in the real world. Continually do mundane tasks to root you in this dimension too, otherwise, you can be inordinately subject to addiction. It's hard to know what is true when you are not in your body and you don't even know that.

Fire/Air– Everything is strategic for you. You look like the general on the hill watching the battle. You take nothing personally so that you can always change immediately and profoundly. Perhaps nothing matters to you more than this. Yet, you don't want that just for yourself. You align with it so that it will be available to all. Ultimately our survival depends upon it.

Red flag: Yikes! Everyone is afraid of this one. You like change so much that you are willing to use any means to engage it. This sometimes calls in your darker instincts and violence. Remember, "The end does not justify the means." Lighten up. You adore a good time. Make sure your schedule is full with those moments. The rest will work itself out.

Fire/Ethers– You are a finely honed antenna. You hear your Spirit and you cannot conceive of anything but following it. Because of this you will always have energy at the ready. Use it wisely.

Red flag: When you hear your Spirit that clearly it is difficult to realize that it is just a part of you. You ego is not in charge of it. Sometimes you will fall into that territory. It's all a part of divine order and timing. When you over-exceed the boundaries and circumstances, stop. Apologize. Start over. You are gifted at starting over.

Water– **Fire** brings warmth to **Water's** coolness. Sometimes it opens up gorgeous vistas that **Water** did not dare to seek out. It lightens the mood and therefore the load.

Red flag: When fear is in charge here, it is a dictator. It will change any circumstances to justify any action. Watch for extremes of expression and thought. These are vital clues: "It always happens like this. That's never going to work." Find some fun instead of obsessing. Salsa dancing may be your best friend.

Water/Water– Shy and introverted are natural territories for the **Water/Water** being. **Fire** brings you out into the world in spite of yourself. You have so much love to give, it is never ending.

Red flag: You are trying so hard to see the truth—so much so that you keep trying when you ought to stop and give it a rest. You are relentless, obsessive, and lost in your own drama. Find somebody with bigger problems than yours and help guide them. You will find your way too.

Water/Earth– Action. You are called to act again and again. Fortunately, you usually do it with spot-on timing, grace and ease. You love a win/win situation. You will make great things.

Red flag: You can become judgmental and exclusive. Work at inviting everybody into your visions. Trust that your loved ones will be fine. Do not overreach your authority in their lives. Find a hobby.

Water/Fire– Look at how bold and sassy you are! You love beauty. It loves you because you are appreciative. On a good day, there is nothing you take for granted. Your innate sensitivity breeds a keen awareness that you focus on the positive.

Red flag: You don't really like anybody. You want to but they drive you crazy. If they just did things the right way it would be different. You would be different. You are probably right as far as logic goes, yet logic only goes so far. In the realm of the heart where you are destined to truly live, right and wrong are trumped by unconditional acceptance. Start now. Love everything, even when you don't like it.

Water/Air–
Have you ever noticed that you usually second guess yourself a lot? That is about to change. You feel braver. You walk faster. You start the morning earlier. It's not that you are really any more certain, it's just that you are truly excited to see the outcome of your best efforts now. Good for you.

Red flag: Sometimes you play the martyr. When you add **Fire** to your Imprint, be careful that you don't justify belittling your significance in favor of everyone else. Be magnanimous. It is an easy place for you to go. Be as generous with yourself as with anyone else.

Water/Ethers–
You have raised intuition and telepathy to an art form. Use it respectfully. There are worlds upon worlds for you to open up and explore. Everything enriches you. Deep down your in utero memories are close to the surface. Allow them. The experience of pure union with all lifeforce endears you to everything.

Red flag: Be a guide. Be a mentor. Just don't lord it over anybody. Offer your wisdom freely and let go. Whenever possible, walk away. Never forget that no matter what it looks like, ultimately everybody knows what is best for them. This matter is best left between them and their Spirits. Physician, heal thyself.

Air–
You are so much fun, everybody says it. Why were you hiding your light under a bushel basket until now? Share the wealth.

Red flag: Sometimes you play with the truth, not maliciously—you simply want to see how things work. People are not a science experiment for you. Honor their feelings above all else. Slow down. Remember the Golden Rule.

Air/Air–
Your curiosity knows no bounds and why should it? You boldly go into the unknown and bring back treasures that were undreamed of before now.

Red flag: Unrealistic. Reckless. So distracted you lose purpose and perspective. Dancing is a superb outlet for you.

Air/Earth–
You are a pioneer. Thank goodness you do not live on outside validation. You are brave and bold enough to lend a hand in the most dramatic of circumstances. Isn't that what help really is.

Red flag: How do you know what you know? Ask yourself this religiously. Bring beginner's mind to it every time. You are susceptible to dark subterranean motivations when you don't even know it. Why go there? Keep objective friends and ways around you at all times to keep you honest.

Air/Fire– You want to lead. Maybe you will never be a CEO but you want to be in charge of something and this is a marvelous instance. You can be clear, direct and fresh-faced. Even better than that, you rarely take things personally. Wherever you place your initiative, it will bring forth unexpected miracles.

RED FLAG: When the attention is not on you, you get lost. When no one is following your grand schemes, you can lose track of what's really important. Even if you travel a lot, cultivate a safe, peaceful and nourishing home. Keep it simple. Have an oasis there that is only for you. Meditate until you find your way back.

Air/Water– Now you have found the underlying motivations that make things worthwhile for you. You cannot pick your destiny by logic or emotion alone. You must find honest passion. It is inexplicable and right on. It wants to lead you. Surrender to it.

RED FLAG: Be realistic. Most of the time you view this as a drag on your day. But play with it. Lean into it. Sometimes you have to lead with your weak suit. It is the way of mastery in all things. Make sure you have a good laugh about it too.

Air/Ethers– It is easy for you to cheerfully surrender to your Spirit. Do it. Act upon it. The time and the courage are with you now. Believe.

RED FLAG: Even if you are saving the world, neglecting your body will bring you down. Stamina is not your strong suit. When you embrace the truth of that you will find enough inspiration to make your health a priority . . . so that you can do and be anything. Eat your vegetables.

Ethers– You were conceived in love. You were born with love. You are made up of love. Of this you are certain. Share that with all parts of yourself, then share that unfailingly with others. They court your optimism and so do you.

RED FLAG: Doubt makes liars of us all. You hate that. You are overly dramatic and excessive at times in everything. It is a bold way to embrace life, yet sometimes utterly inefficient. Find a clear, positive foundation. Focus on it with all your heart.

Ethers/Ethers– Wow. That may be your most apt description. You are a visionary, a futurist, a chef, a pilot and a healer. How do all of these things come together? You answer the need when it knocks at your door. That is a thrill beyond description. Wow.

RED FLAG: You have so many horses, you don't know how to marshal them. Your body is like a house with many unruly toddlers. You want to give them all-out freedom but nothing is getting done. Establish regular mealtimes and a bath at the end of every day. Go calmly into the dreamtime every night. You need to bring full presence there instead of scattered stimuli.

Ethers/Earth– Pick your vocation well. Likely it will define you physically and Spiritually. You have so much to give. Receive equally back from your choices and you will never be without energy.

RED FLAG: Sometimes there is a spooky loneliness that travels with this Imprint. Explaining it doesn't make it go away. Learn to live with it. Just choose to accept that you will not always be understood. Appreciate that about you. Never turn on yourself. Be free. Be happy. Whatever joins you there will be of like Spirit.

Ethers/Fire– If you had more patience you would be running the solar system. Instead you are in charge of happiness. Revel in that. When you do more of your bliss you grow lifeforce itself. What could be more spectacular!

>   *Red flag:* Bored? Of course you are. Believe it or not, that could be a sign of a full life. You have bypassed no feelings so even boredom finds you. Welcome it. Never turn away. Study it. Remember the adage, "Keep your friends close and your enemies closer."

Ethers/Water– When you get dreary, **Fire** will perk you up. It brings unexpected delight. Then you have to break out of pessimism. Stand in the sunlight. It reminds you why we are primarily emotional beings.

>   *Red flag:* When you focus on the negative nothing deters you. All of your talents get mired there. What gets you unstuck? Let go of old emotions. Go for a walk. Play with animals. Periodically do things that are just light, silly and fun.

Ethers/Air– When there are pressing needs, you will answer. You will answer immediately with the full force of your gifts at the ready. Armed with **Fire**, the world finds you bold, adventurous, entertaining and simultaneously healing. That seems like an impossible combination until now.

>   *Red flag:* You are lost in the details. You are so lost you don't even know what the big picture and the details are. Forget it. Start over. Meditation is a life-long ally. Never lose track of it. Never venture far away from it. Its emptiness will lead you back to the Center Stillness.

SUMMARY: Adding **Fire** reminds you that life brings you the choice of joy. If you accept the invitation no matter the current prevailing mood, you will create more joy, more lifeforce - just plain more. This is a constant. You can believe in it and right now you want to believe. Go for it. What happens by adding the **Water** Elemental to the following Birth Imprints:

Earth– These two are lovers, forever in a slow luxurious embrace. Appreciate life and all its gifts. That is the meaning that you couldn't name. Immerse yourself in it. Hot springs were made for you.

>   *Red flag:* Share your affections with as many as possible, otherwise you grow rigid and judgmental. You need to be exposed to other points of view. Even if you reject them they will stretch you beyond your own capabilities.

Earth/Earth– You revel in comfort. You like your things. It's not that you are materialistic per se, it is that they remind you of the love that you have given and received. You are loyal. You will never forget a friend. You are stability embodied.

>   *Red flag:* Generally, the world moves too fast for you. You feel judged and misunderstood. Your values are not esteemed by all. This upsets you more than anything. Learn to love people in this perfect moment of their journey. It will help you to know they are a work-in-process. So are you. There, it is easier already.

Earth/Fire– Hurrah! The people around you just let off a collective cheer. They know well that you know how to be in charge. You seldom stammer or hesitate. And now, you just added compassion to your modus operandi. Well done.

> RED FLAG: Be fair. No favorites. Let the natural cycles of life guide you in your priorities, values and subsequent actions. Your heart wants to open. Trust it.

Earth/Water– Is this a flood? Yes! It will fertilize something magical. Nobody knows for sure what that is yet your willingness is utterly creative. Even when it seems moody, act upon it. We need more emotional intelligence in our lives.

> RED FLAG: It is a fine line but don't be too moody. The rule of thumb is to let your emotions come and go at will. They will always change. Change with them instead of obsessing on your old moods. Now you are an expressive artist. Paint your life in all colors and poetry.

Earth/Air– Hurrah for **Water**! You will call upon your left and right brain with amazing affability and fluency. Your corpus callosum rules.

> RED FLAG: Life is not a theory. It is a complete and ever-growing experience. Engage it or you will deaden your gifts. It may be hard for you to tell when you are not fully present (because your mind is so full). The test is to live through your senses. Go naked. Feast ridiculously. Savor aromas. Cuddle a new baby. Just focus on your senses and your body innately leads the way.

Earth/Ethers– You have the seeds of greatness within you. It is unlikely that you will be famous enough for the world to know this. However, there will be at least one or two people who will be so uplifted by your love that they will transmute unneeded suffering. There is no way to logically prove this, which is fine, because you don't need proof—you are living it.

> RED FLAG: Obsession is a dark, sometimes well visited, corner in your world. Accept the truth of this and choose not to judge it. Let go of judgment. And when you judge the times you didn't let go, just let go. Surrender to the biggest picture possible. Not only can you do it, you were made for it. It would be silly to martyr your magnificence to moods.

Fire– **Fire** and **Water** do not always know how to work together. Fair enough. Start off their friendship by playing together. When you don't know what else to do, enjoy yourself. Smile. That usually attracts what you truly need.

> RED FLAG: You are so dramatic that you lose track of the truth. And once you start that cycle, you live it and over-live it dangerously. Whether you want to or not, calm down. Get back into your body. Breathe deeper. Before you react, take a breath. Say nothing, at least at first. All will be revealed to you.

Fire/Fire– Sometimes you need calm. Even when you do not believe that, you are welcoming in the calm that your life needs so that you can grow peace. From that, you can do anything in love instead of anger.

> RED FLAG: You need to check in with a higher authority, your Spirit, your enduring philosophy, with your own Center Stillness. Whatever that is, make a date to meet frequently regardless of mood or desire. Find your guiding light or be lost in causes that you cannot fulfill.

Fire/Earth– You know the rules of life. You play them well. You manifest successfully. Now you are adding the variable of unexpected love wherever it finds you. Receive it and be renewed.

> *Red flag:* Don't forget to have fun. Be spontaneous. Be a child. Otherwise, things will be deadly serious for you and who wants to be deadened.

Fire/Water– You know how to look into somebody's eyes and recognize them. You boldly offer acceptance where no one else dares to go. You follow your heart yet you are not reckless. You do it with a constancy of love that renews itself.

> *Red flag:* You did not resolve everything from your childhood. While this is true of everyone, you must be careful or you will be subconsciously nursing old hurts that will keep attracting replays of your struggles. Resolve to love your family. You are forever bonded. You can appreciate that in and of itself or you can get angrier and angrier. It is your choice.

Fire/Air– You learn things so quickly almost nobody can track it. When you add Water to this your memory grows keen. You retain wisdom for exactly the right moments. You know how to flow with the unexpected and let it nurture your "adventurer" considerately.

> *Red flag:* You want to stay friends with everybody forever. When you are in balance, people come and go around you all the time. When you are distracted by chaos, you suddenly look to key loved ones to save you. After all, you would do it for them. Co-dependency by any other name is just as deadly.

Fire/Ethers– Whatever you do, you want to do it with play. You want to leave your mark upon the world so that others will remember the preciousness of everything. Love is a way of life and you can't live without it.

> *Red flag:* You have so much energy you must be careful not to squander it. Wasting life—even an abundance of it—throws away love and respect. Take care of yourself so that every breath is filled with love and focuses on what you truly adore.

Water– Choose to belong with this world. You can nurture anything. Volunteer. Give freely. You have more than enough heart for everything.

> *Red flag:* You are inordinately influenced by others. When that is your choice, be decisive and clear about it. Most of the time you don't notice it. You leak lifeforce on so many desperate causes that you have nothing left over. This infuriates your family (loved ones) who are waiting for the connection that only you and they can have.

Water/Water– Water water everywhere. Whenever so much energy is relentlessly focused in one area, we need that healing. Be alone with yourself and listen to what you must be for your own destiny. Feel it and it will be so.

> *Red flag:* Know yourself. Otherwise everybody's opinions will define your life and you will never know it. You are lost and you do not know how to balance yourself. Listen to nature. It is your finest role model.

Water/Earth– The Goddess is rich in you. Be fertile. Enjoy simple things. Open your heart, speak your truth and all will be blessed.

Red flag: You probably have mother issues. Resolve to be the parent that you always wanted to have when you were a lost misunderstood child. Just accept your hurts and shortcomings as the inevitable marks of life. They do not make you lesser, though you have old thoughts that tell you so. Choose to believe in something finer. Feel it. Make it so.

Water/Fire– Now you have the motivation to dredge up your deepest unresolved pain. While it won't be pretty, you know that and you accept it. You are ready to lavish unconditional love and trust upon every single part of you. You will never give up.

Red flag: Your home still reflects your early strife, even though you don't realize it. Be truly creative in your own space. Make what pleases you and reflects your most honest beliefs, desires and needs. Play with color a lot.

Water/Air– You bring inexplicable magic to the mundane. You share that even when you don't realize it. Be attached to nothing you think or feel. You must change like every breeze and every wave.

Red flag: When you are overly sentimental, you attach to concepts. Resolve to keep letting go of beliefs. Regularly ask yourself, "Is this what I love?" You will have to continually create your beliefs all life long.

Water/Ethers– Do what you can do with the most love possible. Let go of judging whether or not your actions are big enough or grand enough. Love as perfectly as possible whatever is offered to you in this moment. Release all other outcomes.

Red flag: You are so moody, no one wants to talk to you. So why don't you speak up first? Find a way to confide in people who are truly understanding and healing. Never attach to their opinions. Just keep accepting and then releasing your moods. Your job is to love from a clear space.

Air– You like to bring together opposites. It fascinates you. In your heart you trust that opposites are not warring factions but complements on a full spectrum of healing. This delights you so much that you will meet and have friends everywhere.

Red flag: Judgment. Judgment. Judgment. Sometimes when you don't understand you just arbitrarily judge. You give it a label whether it deserves it or not. Once you pass judgment, you seldom have the patience to revisit this assessment. Meditate frequently. It will spontaneously create a clear void in your mind. From there you will attract unexpected inexplicable wisdom.

Air/Air– You are enchanted by everything. You change, you grow, at a moment's notice. You forgive anything and you love to connect people of great differences.

Red flag: You have the attention span of a house-fly. You decide even before you fully view a situation, how much energy and acceptance you will give it. You rarely listen completely and you miss so many treasures. Learn to say, "I didn't get that. Can you say it again?" By sheer repetition you will learn to listen and flourish.

Air/Earth– You bring loyalty and steadiness to any cause. You know there will be difficulties in any venture; therefore, your equilibrium is not disturbed by problems. You greet them calmly and pause to mull over possible solutions. You rarely miss a helpful idea.

Red flag: Learn to speak up. Be bold enough to initiate what you believe in. You have studied long enough and hard enough. Risk what you have learned to put it to good use. Stop fearing the consequences before you even try.

Air/Fire– Everybody likes you and you know it. You know what to say and how to say it and you mean it. This is a rare quality in a world dominated by advertising.

Red flag: You have endless innovative ideas. But you never really give them a chance. You birth them and then you leave them on others' doorsteps, like abandoned orphans. You haven't "figured out" how to love and nurture your creativity into manifestation. But you're mixing metaphors. You can't "figure out" how to love and nurture your gifts. There are no "gimmicks" to this; just accept that everything coming from you is a treasure. Treat them that way.

Air/Water– You care for everybody, everywhere. What a beautiful gift that is! Compassion is impossible to fake. Either you just are it or not: You are it. It constantly reminds you of how perfect everything is.

Red flag: Resist the temptation to tell people what they feel (even if you DO know what they feel). They deserve the freedom to come to their own emotions and processes, whatever they are. Listen, instead of judge. Everyone is perfect, including you. When you let go of your perceived perfectionism, you will relax easily. So will everyone else.

Air/Ethers– You are holding the space for nothing less than global peace. You know it must be and you believe in it utterly. Everything you do connects to a transpersonal harmony. You are acting upon utopia.

Red flag: Detach. Detach. Detach. If you decide for somebody else what peace looks like for them, that's not peace—that is violence. Honor the self-determining power of every individual. When you get distracted judging their choices, stop. Breathe. At the core, something in you is not free. Let it out. That is peace.

Ethers– You genuinely are a different person with everyone you meet. For you, this is honest. It is your gift to offer intimacy at whatever level someone else opens to it. Even better than that, you can constantly shift according to how you all are evolving.

Red flag: Relax. When you get overly serious, calm yourself. Drop your shoulders. Stretch. Do whatever kind things you can do to let go of negative emotions as soon as you are aware of them; otherwise you become overly judgmental and unable to change. Doesn't sound like much fun and at the core, you love fun.

Ethers/Ethers– You have so many abilities there is no way to track them all. Yet one of your vocations is children and encouraging them to stay innocent. You deeply appreciate the magnificent potential in every being and you insist upon seeing that first and foremost in everyone.

Red flag: You are so concerned with people as a "project" you forget to listen to them one-on-one. Your own family and friends know this. They get frustrated and when they do, you get hurt. You distance yourself even further. It is a challenge for you to maintain healthy long-term deep relationships. Maybe you should start with a dog.

Ethers/Earth– You adore nature in all its forms. You can spend all day rock hunting. You can lie on the beach without moving for hours at a time. You learn from all forms of life. Because of this you are enriched beyond anything any school normally offers.

Red flag: You are scared for the future of the human species. You get overly and assuredly pessimistic. Stop. This can attract a never-ending cycle of self fulfilling prophecies. When you do not know how to hope, go in nature. Ask 4-leggeds and winged ones how they manage to be so perfect in the face of possible extinction.

Ethers/Fire– Life is not a concept to you. It is an open heart given to you over and over again. You must give back. You are utterly pledged to this and if you have fun in the process, all the better.

Red flag: You get unreasonable when people don't do what you want fast enough. You want so much. You want the best. "The best" is still a judgment. Train your ears to hear them. Breathe through your judgments. They come for your own healing. Love them and let them go as fast as they appear. Well done.

Ethers/Water– You are here to love as deeply and as profoundly as possible. You want to lose yourself in love. Ego of any kind does not impress you. You want to be subsumed by unconditional love.

Red flag: When things get tough in relationships you get hurt. You withdraw telling yourself that you will not be with that person until they act out of true love. Again, this is a judgment. When you love unconditionally there are no expectations. Just love people where they are at, exactly as they are in this moment. No changes necessary. All is perfect and well.

Ethers/Air– You are utterly adaptable. You are a vehicle of Spirit. You allow yourself to speak and to do what is needed as you feel it. You trust implicitly in divine order and timing. You adore life.

Red flag: It takes a lot to disillusion you but when you are there it takes a lot to get you out. Practice really magnificent affirmations every day all day long. This will wear down your pessimism. Eventually you will believe and when you do you will be a force to be reckoned with, gloriously.

SUMMARY: Adding **Water** is adding emotion. It always increases the potential for love. Concurrently people feel more vulnerable in the presence of more **Water**. The issue here is simple but not easy: Can I keep opening my heart? Adding **Water** adds to the risk and the intimacy.

What happens by adding the **Air** Elemental to the following Birth Imprints:

Earth– Here comes curiosity. Sometimes it's good to stand the world on its head. You're doing that unreservedly and you are learning, learning, learning.

Red flag: You fear everything that you cannot understand. Denial invades all of your perceptions. You believe that you have acute awareness. You have illusions. Ask the people around you to speak their truth. Consider it all and keep learning, learning, learning.

Earth/Earth– You love to know how things work. You love to make things. You love to share that with others. You love everything as long as you get a regular change of scenery and ideas.

Red flag: Your logic eliminates magic. You explain away anything mystical. If anyone around you is open to other dimensions, you secretly fear them. Out loud you judge them. You might seek to destroy their credibility. Eventually life will teach you that everything is possible. Cultivate relationships with wise elders. They may patiently open you up in ways that you could not imagine before.

Earth/Fire– You are on a mission. Actually you may be on several missions. Following your beliefs invigorates you. It brings you in touch with truly remarkable individuals. You love genius. And you gather it around you abundantly.

Red flag: Everybody gets stale at times but you won't admit that. When your heart is not in something you pretend. This damages your psyche more than you will know. From now on, when you do not feel a true calling in something, stop. Just do something else for awhile. Consciously distract yourself with fun. One day, you will wake up and the well will be refilled, but it won't be the same. It will be deeper and more passionate from your learnings.

Earth/Water– By adding **Air** to this Imprint you choose to be as conscious as possible. You like waking up in the morning. The constant newness of life and death revives you. Part of you expects a certain sameness to the seasons, the Sun, the Moon and the Earth. Another part of you continually asks, "What if . . .?" Imagination is born.

Red flag: You wouldn't think this is possible, but you continually fritter away your massive amounts of energy on frivolous amusements. If you realized this you would staunch the bleeding, you would change your mind, and you would focus on learning what enhances your life. But deep down you are feeding your own fears and you don't even know it. They are more than happy to quietly run your life in ways that invisibly scatter your purpose. Try this: At the end of every day, ask yourself, "What have I done? What have I been?" Make a simple list. No need to judge it; in fact, wholeheartedly agree to accept whatever is on the list. Just witness it. After awhile you will see the "invisible" footprints of your defenses in the patterns of distracted activities that leave you depleted. Talk to all the parts of yourself, and change.

Earth/Air– You love to offer people what you have learned because life is so exciting. You are fascinated by almost everything on the Earth. Continually, you discover endless things that deserve your awe. Happily, you share them with others to the upliftment of all.

Red flag: You can do anything and sometimes that is to your discredit. Open up your heart. When it guides you, it automatically puts parameters of compassion, acceptance and love upon all your potentials. Parts of you have forgotten that this way of life even exists. Remember. Even if it is painful opening your heart, it is short term suffering. Living without an open heart is constant, long-term struggle.

Earth/Ethers– You excitedly look for every chance to tell stories of wonder and magnificence. Perhaps more than anything, you want everybody to feel what you absolutely inherently know: People are divine. Life is the expression of Spirit. We all can join in that in ever growing wonder. Everything in your life proves that you are a co-creator with it. You heal extremely well. Literally, you can make anything happen even when you are asleep. Now, more than anything, you want every human on Earth to know the magic that you know.

Red flag: Sharing beliefs is tricky. Sharing beliefs passionately is dangerous. Sharing beliefs insistently is life threatening. None of these truisms has to prove true, yet, in the story of humans they often have. Do not tread over people's free will. You are a natural storyteller. You like to honor the history/herstory of humans. Honor it by freely acknowledging the "mistakes" recorded there by not repeating them.

Fire– You are a party just waiting to happen. Celebrate life before it's gone, is your motto. Every day, you pass that on to as many people as possible. Now that is an enduring legacy.

Red flag: You push the limits, and that is on a good day. On a rough day, you trample them. You might repeatedly risk health and safety. If you are going to do that, do it consciously instead of blindly. Do it in a way that actually increases lifeforce. Your friends will thank you for it.

Fire/Fire– Power is your first and last name. It is because you wake up every day (literally) and see how life moves, dances, and shapes things. You are utterly fascinated; you can't keep your eyes off of this. This potent breathing vision utterly creates your reality. You know what needs to be done and why and when.

Red flag: A beneficent dictator is still a dictator. Repeat this to yourself every hour of every day. Let it seep through your skin until it is in your heart. Judge nothing. Let its truth guide you where your own misplaced priorities cannot go. P.S. Have you ever tried Chi Gong?

Fire/Earth– We met you the other day. You shook our hands while looking us deeply in the eye. You remembered our names. Even when you were doing other things you were connected to us. Sometimes you even felt our needs before we did. Thank you for bringing together all levels of life to all people as often as you can. Perhaps no one is more dedicated than you, and while you didn't ask for this recognition, it fuels you. You secretly delight in it and it brings you smiles on rainy days.

Red flag: Liking and loving people "in theory" is not truly liking and loving anything. If you truly love someone you act upon it even when you don't realize consciously you are, it's built into your instincts from your deepest most constant healings. Let go of being afraid of the constant lurking shadows of the human species. Jump in. Get dirty. Love unreservedly. You will know when you are truly loving because its forms will ever change and deepen in spite of yourself.

Fire/Water— Are you a lawyer? A mediator? An activist? In advertising? Even those of you that said "no" are stunned. Truth resonates through our bodies whenever it is spoken. You may not be employed by any of these professions but parts of you do them regardless. You stand up for truth. You insist that all be accountable for fairness and equality. You want everybody to know that we must take care of each other above all else. (Now wouldn't that make a great advertising campaign?)

> *Red flag:* Learn how to slow down without completely stopping. Of course you want everything that you want right now, and when that doesn't happen instantly, you sometimes take all your toys and go home and refuse to play with the other boys and girls. That just means you are left out of all the fun. Learn to breathe and target it to specific parts of your body. When you are confused, breathe and see out of your third eye. When you are violently impatient, breathe out of your lowest abdomen (and do nothing else but that for a few moments). When fear holds you captive, light up the bottoms of your feet with prana. Tingle your toes.

Fire/Air— Naturally you are entertainer. Probably a comic too. You possess a knack for ferreting out the underlying truth as it is happening. Even better yet, you fearlessly give it voice. We like learning this way because it is quick, direct and we feel your underlying love.

> *Red flag:* Will you never stop talking? We hope that quick directness shows you how much we truly love you. Receive it abundantly again and again. Befriend silence, too.

Fire/Ethers— We were taking bets the other day. Most of us agreed that in your past lifetimes, you have mostly been a magician. No wonder you are so undeniably talented now. Everyone admires your creativity. We all want to learn how to be artists like you and not like you. That is the compliment you have earned from us.

> *Red flag:* If you only share your enthusiasm without your full yet open heart, you will degrade to passing on your judgments. Listen to yourself when you talk. Can you reach out and touch pure feeling in them? You will know when you can because you will come back with compassion in your grasp. If not, stop talking. Take a walk around the block. Better yet, take a walk around the lake. Start over with your heart in your words and your ways.

Water— You are a forever-child. Your inescapable innocence reminds us all of why we are alive. It **shows** us why are deeply, passionately in love with life, at the core. And you gave us all this just when you said, "Good morning . . ..."

> *Red flag:* When you are confused by life, don't just STAY there. Do whatever it takes to move on. That will change everything. You don't believe that right now but you will after you have a change of scenery or a quiet breath away from the maddening crowd.

Water/Water— Ultra sensitive, that's you. When you bravely peek out of your shell and tell us how you feel, we are almost unbelievably honored. You are always braver than you look.

Red flag: When you are hurt, stop. Immediately take whatever steps are necessary to heal it. If you don't know what that is, it is because you are swimming in your own pain. Take a deep breath. Speak up. Put words to what you are experiencing. Trusting the truth of that can bridge you to new and different life. Trust that.

Water/Earth– You can care for anything. Nurturance is bred in your soul. Thank you for opening up that depth to the rest of us. We feel safe enough to be the big brave explorers that we want to be, now.

Red flag: You admire almost everybody else, except yourself. We give you no kudos here for poor self esteem. In old times, some cultures saw that as a sign that you were focusing on others first, and that was loving and admirable. At this time in evolution upon the Earth, that quality doesn't work. Love isn't love when you always leave you out of it. Relentlessly include yourself in your care and see how quickly magic resurrects itself in your presence.

Water/Fire– When you look at us, you show us how deeply you care. The amount of attention you freely offer says it all. And the fact that you can do this with virtually everybody and anybody only increases your magnificence.

Red flag: Be at peace. It's nice that you have strong emotions but when you obsess on them you strangle their passion and replace it with addiction. Dramatic enough for you? Regularly schedule quiet times. During them, think nothing. This will reset your metabolism and allow your innate body wisdom to take over and calm down when needed. You know how to grow peace. You just forget sometimes to do it.

Water/Air– You are so likeable you could be a puppy. Everybody wants to tell you their stories and they do. You know how to keep their secrets safe and their ways honored.

Red flag: Let go of double-thinking everything. Nothing will ever get done this way. Is that what you really want? Do you want to live your life with your finger on the PAUSE button? Make a decision. When you do, find a quick and happy way to reward yourself. Pretty soon you will balance your gut and your mind ambidextrously.

Water/Ethers– You truly care. You will live and die caring as deeply as is possible. With the addition of **Air**, you are resolved to share that with as many people as possible.

Red flag: No dream or scheme is grand enough for you. You design and redesign your projects endlessly. All of your energy is knotted up in the R & D phase. Love your dreams enough to birth them. Trust the amazing people around you. Tell them about your obsessive perfectionism. Delegate the manifesting of your fine dreams to them.

Air– You love to learn. It thrills you that infinite ideas are knocking at your door. Your are fearless in studying anything. Because of this you can relate to anybody, anywhere, anytime.

Red flag: When you talk to people remember to *include them* in the conversation. Sometimes talk. Sometimes listen. The give and receive of this honors you more than constantly thinking out loud.

Air/Air–

You are a translator of, and for, life. If anyone doesn't understand something, you stop and repeat the appropriate words until they "aha!" That is your reward. Nothing fulfills you more than banishing unneeded ignorance.

Red flag: You are scatteredness embodied, except that you are not embodied at the moment. You are **Air** blowing through the theories of everything without ever touching the ground. You think big and probably do little. Yes, yes, even now you are denying this. Let go of using words as your first and only means of expressing your energy. Say nothing, do something.

Air/Earth–

You are probably a scientist, aren't you? Some of you are grinning to beat the band. The rest of you are deep in thought, "How did they come up with that? How does that work? Where does the information come from? Do they know me?" We rest our case.

Red flag: There is nothing you can't invent. You are innovation embodied when you allow yourself generously. Testing and retesting your possibilities isn't inventing, it is stalling. Call it like it is and you can, and will, change. That is your true strength. Go with it.

Air/Fire–

Creativity is you. Are you an artist? Of course you are. You know how to see things as they are and as they could be simultaneously. You can sculpt anything out of lifeforce.

Red flag: Stop living on Facebook. It is lovely that you want to connect with everyone everywhere but are you connecting with YOU? If you are, then you are making dreams come true. If you are not, then you are dancing around the edges like a wannabe. No need for that, your visions are glorious. Organize a party and do them.

Air/Water–

You care about everything that has ever been said. That means that you will learn from every story and you will unswervingly share that with everyone, everywhere. No effort is spared in this. You give your heart to learning/evolving, so that no one needs to be hurt or humiliated.

Red flag: Judge nothing. Hard isn't it? Let go of judging your judgments, too. Accept everything. Even when you aren't in the mood, unconditionally trust that everything happens for a perfect, divine reason. You can't stop that, nor would you really want to, right?

Air/Ethers–

You are a genius. Even when nobody can figure out what your genius is, it lives on. You will prove this to be true because you try so bravely to make it so. Your efforts will reap huge rewards. Watch. You'll see.

Red flag: Understanding comes AFTER the experience. Though you desperately imagine otherwise, understanding what pain is going to drop down on you will **not** stop pain from ever visiting you. Now that you are reading that, you are sighing. You know the truth when you read it. You have been avoiding life, though you are pretending otherwise. Just jump in before you over-think yourself to death. Jump in. You'll probably fall, but on the bright side, you bounce exceedingly well. (...you didn't know that?...)

Ethers– You actually are both wise and knowledgeable. And when you believe in something you possess and incredible memory and ability to create miracles from what you have understood about life. You are incredibly patient in sharing your wisdom and believe that sharing it expands it.

>   Red flag: You find it extremely hard to relate what you know to real life. Sometimes that is stubborn defensiveness because you are utterly pessimistic about the "real" world. Fortunately you can be easy to distract. This means when you get relentlessly dark you can stop yourself. Visit with friends. Do small unexpected things. Engage in heart-pumping sports. You will change your mind to a lighter brighter place. You always do.

Ethers/Ethers– Genius. Unexpected. Witty. Forthright. Expansive. All true and all you.

>   Red flag: Some people know so much about some things they don't know how to simply lead a regular fulfilling life. That is you. At times, you relate to nothing and no one and vice versa. And this is a shame because even your quirky facts have something valuable to share. Get out of your head. Every day do some conscious movement: Yoga, Tai Chi, bodywork, etc. You just need to be reminded that you have a perfectly beautiful body to inhabit and enjoy.

Ethers/Earth– Life has brought you many adventures. Even the ones that you didn't like made you strong, charismatic, healing and wise. You are so wise that you prefer to act upon what you know instead of talking about it. When you role model for others however, do speak up. Demonstrate and then explain. It will simply add to your wisdom.

>   Red flag: Go ahead and believe, believe in whatever you can. Start small and simply. That is something you can build upon and you will be forever grateful for that. Constant doubt is not a way of life. It is a denial of life. Expand upon your talents. Let go of wasting them.

Ethers/Fire– You love to be enthusiastic, which means that you are constantly in rapture. Everything piques your curiosity. However you focus on the things that drive your passions. You want to make a difference in the world and you are.

>   Red flag: When you fritter your energy away, you lose track of who you are. You don't even remember what you believe in. You find yourself reinventing your life continually which is like reinventing the wheel. Stand up for what you do believe. Be certain of that. Use positive affirmations religiously.

Ethers/Water– You are profound. When you speak you usually talk about what really matters. You honor the people close to you. There is nothing you wouldn't do (that is respectful) to unconditionally support and adore them. This grows your love so much, you are eager to share it with new friends.

>   Red flag: You have so many ideas you don't know what to do. Your mind is a non-stop ping pong game, but you never get to the point. Every morning, meditate. This will clear you. Your mind will embark upon a fresh path. If you need any previous knowledge and wisdom, it will automatically show up when required. Worry about nothing. Every night, immerse yourself in Water (physically and/or psychically) and wash away the day's dirt and think nothing more about it. Go to bed with an open easy heart. Your dreams are made up of magic; tomorrow's morning meditation will show you.

Ethers/Air– No matter what, you can make anyone smile. You are so skilled at finding delight in every corner, in every disguise, that you brighten anyone's day. That jazzes you so much, you are endless energy. You dream and vision constantly.

>   **RED FLAG:** You have a hard time getting to sleep at night, don't you? Some people simply do not know how to wind down. Picture this: Inside your head is an on/off switch. Play with it; it works really well. Once you get the hang of it, only use it when you need it. At night, hit the "off" switch. Revel in the silence. Listen to Starlight. Fall blissfully asleep and awaken refreshed. Once you have the hang of this, use the on/off switch as needed in particular situations. It is a gift.

SUMMARY: When you are in your body and balanced and call upon extra **Air**, you receive breath, objectivity and ultimately, spontaneous ways to link body and Spirit. When you are afraid, extra **Air** enlivens distractions and defenses. Don't be put off by this. They need attention too. Just remember, breathing prana may be the fastest, most complete way to open your heart. That is the doorway to everything that you are. Affirm it.

What happens by adding the Ethers Elemental to the following Birth Imprints:

Earth– What you don't know can help you. Adding **Ethers** to **Earth** brings mystery and multidimensional grace and ease. It explains the core "why" without the need for words. **Earth** Imprints love to believe without thinking about it. They act upon the **Ethers** beautifully.

>   **RED FLAG:** You are discombobulated aren't you? We can tell by the way you are spinning around and gasping. Relax. Adding new ways of life will disorient you. Accept that. It's called learning. No need to get all dizzy about it. Do what you do best: Ground. Ask your wise body about this new information. It never lies to you.

Earth/Earth– Practical. Sensible. Real-world AND inspired. You take magic and you put it into everything right before our eyes. Some people wouldn't believe it except that they are seeing it.

>   **RED FLAG:** You believe what you believe. Changing doesn't dishonor your beliefs. It can expand them so that you can believe even more magnificence. You know that don't you? Ok. Go directly to your Guides and your Guardian Angel. Don't leave until you understand a fresh perspective. Trust.

Earth/Fire– Some saints go down in a blaze of glory. Not you. You are here to embody greatness. You know that so perfectly that you are going to stick around a long time to see the next wonders, and the next, and the next . . .

>   **RED FLAG:** Having a superior attitude just means that when you fall you will fall a long ways. This is unnecessarily painful and you know it. When you see it in others you are quick to spot it and report it. Turn that blazing insight on you. When you get moody, focus on what part of you you've neglected. Of course it's angry. Take time. Give every part of you attention. That is worthwhile.

Earth/Water– Your antennae are directly linked to the Earth and all nature. You feel it because you love Her even when you don't understand Her. You are blessedly guided by the everyday mysteries of life and you stand in awe and gratitude of everything.

> *Red flag:* Stop being suspicious about what you don't know. Open up your mind as well as your heart. You know what they say about the mind: Like a parachute, it operates best when it is open. You know this. You believe this. You just forgot for a little bit. Start over and open up.

Earth/Air– There is always something new to be explored and you are always there to initiate it. We love how you are undeterred by challenge, difficulty, dirt, moods—even impossibilities. You have the most undefeated temperament of anyone we have ever met.

> *Red flag:* If you can't prove it, it isn't so. That means love doesn't exist. That means beauty is an illusion. That means that spontaneous healing cannot be. Well that doesn't sound like an Earth you want to inhabit does it? Change the parameters of your beliefs. When things happen outside of your box, instead of saying, "No," train yourself to smile and say, "Maybe . . ."

Earth/Ethers– Wow, look at the Spirit families around you! Talk about standing room only. Congratulations. You are supremely guided. You have developed your instincts into intuition. Act upon them. Even when they are interruptive your Angels are not. All is well, and then some.

> *Red flag:* Wanting to believe doesn't get you any closer to owning it. They call it "a leap of faith" very aptly. Go ahead and jump. You will soar. You will find things that not even imagination hinted about.

Fire– There is no way to define the spontaneous miracles that you pulled out of your pocket. They are an act of nature. And it is natural to you. You insist upon it therefore it is.

> *Red flag:* Sometimes common sense just isn't that common. So take your extra sensory perceptions and grow some common sense. You will live longer, healthier and happier.

Fire/Fire– You cannot be contained. Wherever you go, happiness and wildness follow. You bring out the unexpected wonder in everybody and everything. Nobody could be more delighted than you.

> *Red flag:* You hate it when things don't go your way. But what is your way? Remember, when you have desires, they are yours. They belong to you and they are for you. YOU. That is less frustrating. You are absolutely positively in charge of you and way more than capable of satisfying your own desires. Keep it that way.

Fire/Earth– You delight in the little things and in the big things. You are going to spend the rest of your life showing the rest of us how to appreciate beauty and grace. Nobody knows better than you that we are already in paradise. Thanks for the reminder.

Red flag: We heard you were having a hissy fit. Again! Nobody is capable of truly living up to anybody else's vision, especially yours. And that is the best news of the day. Nobody is **supposed** to live up to anybody else's vision. Here is a news flash: You get those spectacular flashes of "how it is supposed to be" because that is how it is supposed to be, for you. You are meant to live your vision. Stop blaming everybody else. Anger is passion turned upside down. Set it back on its feet and get on with acting on your vision now.

Fire/Water–
Does everybody know how deeply you feel? The lucky ones do.

Red flag: Speak up! And if people didn't understand you, take a breath, close your eyes, ask for your inner wise Spirit to tell you another way to explain it to your loved ones. Remember that when you get frustrated, ultimately, you are the one that pisses you off. Now you are empowered again. Change. It is what you do best and most often. Change how you link with others and be gracious.

Fire/Air–
When we send ambassadors to outer space, you will be the first one. You enter every situation confident that you have the beliefs and philosophy needed to serve kindly and justly in any situation. Equally respectful, is your Motto.

Red flag: You talk so fast and leave out so many (boring) details, that hardly anybody understands you. It makes it difficult for people to believe in you. That is when you start doubting that you are divinely guided. That's pretty dramatic isn't it? Just slow down. Before you communicate, take a breath and listen to your body and honor it. While you speak, listen to yourself. Make sure you make sense. If not, apologize and start all over again. Practice does make perfect.

Fire/Ethers–
There is nothing you cannot figure out and that is because you don't figure out anything—you instinctively let Spirit whisper in your ear. It delights you to share that abundantly.

Red flag: You understand so much because you focus all your energy on that, and not everybody can. Understand that and you will change in ways that makes life easier.

Water–
You are here to embrace all healing possible. You will feel uncomfortable. You will get used to it. The rewards of freedom and love make it all worthwhile.

Red flag: Memory can be a tricky thing. When you are remembering that you are union and Spirit embodied, you are complete. When you remember every slight ever handed to you, be careful, don't replay it until you are ready to put your arms around it, love it, and let it go. This is a cardinal rule of healing. When you feel badly, immediately meet it with absolute love and set it free.

Water/Water–
Sometimes life is too much for you. Perfect! Share it with everybody else. You have gifts that may never blossom until you give them away.

Red flag: You can hardly get up from the weight of accumulated emotions. Cleanliness is next to godliness. Resolve to keep your body and your heart clear and pure. Never do this in anger, just with love. Sweep the debris of life from you constantly. Others will learn from this and heal.

Water/Earth— You never forget what is truly important. Your priorities are continually in alignment. You care for everything in your world and everything cares for you. As a bonus, you adore the Spirits of nature.

>   *Red flag:* It is glorious to see the good in everyone's heart. However, don't be fooled. Ask to see the truth of what you need to know. When someone means you harm, it is perfectly fine to know that. After all, it is always nice to have time to duck.

Water/Fire— You are intuition embodied. When you accept that, you are on adventure. We are going with you! This is going to be fun!

>   *Red flag:* Talk about extremes. Up and down. Down and up. You are so capable you can do this: Train yourself to not take everything seriously. Show some healthy discrimination. Ask for your Spirit's guidance continually, even if you think you already know. Your nerves will thank you for this.

Water/Air— Wow. You are so patient. You have time for everyone. Absolutely, you love and treasure every single life.

>   *Red flag:* Sometimes separation happens between your heart and your mouth. You know better but sometimes you say disrespectful things to try and snap people out of their stupor. It rarely works. Refocus that energy on you. That is enlightening. When you do that you will spontaneously say the most loving things at the most loving moments.

Water/Ethers— You are multidimensional. Communication isn't just in words, you have proved that. You say everything you need to in waves of compassion. You are probably an animal communicator.

>   *Red flag:* Welcome back to planet Earth. Did you miss us? You are gone so often that your family moved and you didn't even notice. Living in your own world doesn't protect you, it just gets lonely. Every day, resolve to show a loved one how and why you care. Now that is a brave new world.

Air— You knew it. You are right, and the Aquarian Age is proving it: Nothing is impossible. Whenever you get discouraged, you hear that line from an old movie whispering in your ear, "Something wonderful is happening!" Thanks for showing the rest of us all the places to find the wonder.

>   *Red flag:* You judge everything. Just remember that when you point that finger at someone, four fingers point back at you. It's a good thing you are impatient. That means you won't stick with those old judgments much longer.

Air/Air— You are driven to understand. Luckily you find it often. The rest of us happily follow your lead. It makes all of our lives sweeter and richer.

>   *Red flag:* We have never seen anybody distract themselves so constantly, and sometimes so happily, to even remember what you are about. Before you set out on adventure, take a moment, visualize a few outcomes. Make them vivid. Display them on a big screen. This will motivate you to stay on task. Focus isn't boring, it is a splendid honor and choice.

Air/Earth— If we took a bunch of your friends and put them together in a room, would they be able to talk to each other? Maybe not . . . until you show up and connect the dots.

> **RED FLAG:** You want to take care of your body; you just don't know how to prioritize. Start with this: The greatest riches are paid out in energy. Energy equals health. That helps, doesn't it?

Air/Fire— You are doing grand things. Boldness becomes you. You prosper in the most bizarre circumstances.

> **RED FLAG:** If you would stop telling people what to do you would learn so much more. And that is what really makes you happy. Listen. Give yourself a chance to convert knowledge into wisdom.

Air/Water— You may be the best friend anybody ever had. Loyal. Funny. Daring. Ridiculous. Generous. When you give your heart, you give everything. We are never afraid to bring you a problem to help solve.

> **RED FLAG:** Ever heard of boundaries? Why not? Get some. This doesn't mean that you are shutting people out. It means that you are remembering to honor you too. You get to be one of the great loves of your life.

Air/Ethers— You have been to other realms, haven't you? I see it in your eyes. No wonder you are so happy. We are learning to believe just by being around you.

> **RED FLAG:** It's true that you regularly hear the wisdom of the Ages. News flash: That doesn't mean that all of YOUR words are the same as that golden wisdom. Just in the moment, that probably hurts your feelings. But it breaks you open to greater truths and greater wisdom.

Ethers— You know who you are even when you forget. Your sense of purpose is firm enough to be relaxed. Seldom prone to moods, you remain peaceful, gregarious and comfortable in your own skin.

> **RED FLAG:** When you do question life, you get obsessed. You have a hidden stubborn streak. When uncovered, you are resistant to change, love and support. Your saving grace is that you persevere no matter what. Just keep keeping on and you will be guided miraculously at the perfect moment.

Ethers/Ethers— You have other-worldly talents, yet they are not talents to you, just normal abilities that you practice regularly. You can talk to anybody under the most stressful circumstances. You know how to understand and be understood because of your strong focused energies.

> **RED FLAG:** "Whoops! I hate that when I forget I have a body! Where did I leave it last?" Sound familiar? Secretly, you detest limits, and on a moody day, your body equals limits. Time to heal that break. Love your body. Your Spirit does. Model yourself after that.

Ethers/Earth– There is no form of life that you don't honor. You appreciate everything on the Earth. Your most favorite experiences come when you are quiet and immersed in nature. Lots of epiphanies just land on you then.

> **Red flag:** You don't like humans much, do you? When you look at the destruction on the Earth Mother, you blame humans. You hold a grudge. Stop. You are a human, aren't you? If you hate them, you hate yourself by association. That makes it pretty difficult to wield enough positive energy to co-create a harmonious planet. Act upon acceptance. Just do it.

Ethers/Fire– You have the spotlight. Most everything you have to share is divinely inspiring. When people realize it (and they do) they eat it up. Their lives change. Spontaneous miracles follow you doggedly.

> **Red flag:** When you get discouraged, you get loud about it. You rant so hard even your Angels wear ear plugs. Keep it up. Get it out of your system. Exercise at the same time. Shout, run up and down, but do it with the intention that when you calm down you are going to use your energy in a new way. Ask Spirit for other solutions.

Ethers/Water– Children and innocence find you wherever you go. It is obvious that you live in another world within this one. In your world, great things keep happening. It's the law.

> **Red flag:** Stop trying to save the world. Who put you in charge and said, "YOU have to be the one to set things right?" Pretty egotistical isn't it? Start over. Start every day secure in the knowingness that ultimately all is right. The law is: Great things do keep happening.

Ethers/Air– When people are discouraged, they turn to you. That is when you shine. You can speak to numbers of people easily and spontaneously and you are never at a loss for something happy to pass on. You love seeing people connect with each other in this way.

> **Red flag:** Perseverance. Cultivate perseverance. You got the right ideas, just stay with them until they come true. That is the best investment of your time and energy, wouldn't you say?

SUMMARY: **Ethers** reflects our consciousness back to us. We see it in others. We feel it in animals. We interact with it with the Earth. It is all around us showing us what we are like at the core. **Ethers** are infinite, forever, and unconditional. We have to go beyond the constraints of physical reality to even fathom them. And when we do, everything comes together.

Affirming Complete Union

We can align and evolve with the Elementals in infinite ways forever. That's how it is with anything that lives at the core of life, and the Elementals embody that thoroughly. Even as we talk about this now, the Elementals within speak to each other. They love affirming complete union. While we are learning about them in all parts of our being and doing (and the human specialty is "doing") they realign us. Our spines shift. Our toes wiggle into the Earth (figuratively). Our hearts open. Extra ease affirms us even as we integrate ever-growing challenges within evolution. Every day with every breath, new ways of aligning with the Elementals present themselves. Hint: Consciously open yourself to this as you take in every word here.

The most obvious way of aligning with the Elementals is through aligning with their reflection in others. Up till now, humans have not gotten along with each other well. Yet, that is changing dramatically. Whether we fully recognize it or not, this is because we are evolving together. Our congenital separateness is shifting back into union. Evolution is touching all of us equally.

When that gets difficult, in our human relationships we must go back to our core and affirm that—consciously affirm that each of us is the embodiment of the Elementals and then align with them. So simple. That act of freely going to the core and aligning together reverberates from the core outward to all forms of life and circumstance.

When we feel hurt by our friends' comments we align with the **Water** Elemental. This breeds unconditional love and acceptance. It is not necessary to keep going over the hurt feelings or the exact details or our judgments of them (i.e. "I'm right. He is wrong.") Instead, from the depth of our being, where we ARE the Water Elemental in human form, we just give it up. With all the willingness we can muster (Hint: it's a lost cause trying to judge "how willing" you are, you just go with it as that is its nature.) we freely surrender our hurt to the Water Elemental. Here is what will happen: We become our feelings. The hurt may deepen. All of our energy goes to feeling. The moment that happens our hearts open. It is instinctive, reflexive. Once our hearts open, brooding doesn't stand a chance. We feel everything that has been given to us to feel and then it heals, and we heal. If you start to falter in your willingness, remember, your only job is to align with the **Water** Elemental. This keeps your heart open beyond your individual strength. You are linked to the core of life itself through the **Water**. You and your heart are thoroughly forever encouraged.

You heal. The old emotions have transformed. They are no longer judged so they are no longer abnormally attached to you through pain. They freely go. They freely go because that simply is their true nature. Emotions, like Elementals, just come and go continually in perfect timing and purpose. It is only with humans learning that they pause in their journey briefly. They stop. They separate from life. They unconditionally experience the struggle of the evolving human. And then, no matter what, they slip away. They rejoin life. They renew in some other form because life is always changing. Emotions, the children of the **Water** Elemental, change like the tides. Comforting isn't it? When we realize that, we understand that we do not OWN feelings—never did. In aligning with the **Water** Elemental we live at the core of truth. We are free. "Our" emotions are free. Basking in the all-encompassing acceptance of **Water**, we surrender to the inevitable. We let go of any and all feelings and then we all travel to the Center Stillness and affirm union and freedom.

All of a sudden we lost our hurt. Where did it go? It is so gone we can't quite remember the particulars of it. When we let it go, it let go of us. Give thanks to the **Water** Elemental. Together you have consciously imprinted your body. Whatever you have just released (what was it?) will never return.

That exact pain is freedom. It has gone on to another form of life thankfully. You will never experience those precise hurt feelings again. You are healing and the **Water** Elemental is affirming you. Ultimately, it can be no other way.

Nobody said that you will never feel insulted or picked on again. There perhaps are endless feelings available to humans. Healing and evolution offers us so many faces to know and love. When we heal something, accept that and move on. Keep breathing with **Water**. You will meet other feelings that will challenge you. Accept this too. You and the **Water** Elemental are up to the task.

That is one example of how aligning with the Elementals keeps you balancing and healing. For every challenge in your life, feel its core qualities. Then, match those with the core qualities of the Elementals. Align with that Elemental mentally, emotionally, physically, and spiritually. You and everything you experience are just another exponential wave of LIFEFORCE doing its magnanimous thing in generous perfect timing and order.

So we know that when we are swept away in emotion we can breathe **Water**. There are endless opportunities to connect with **Water** for balancing. We can go swimming. We can run on the beach. Ever just stood in a soft rain? Or we can picture **Water** in our minds-eye and see it clearly washing away our old hurt. We see and feel ourselves as clear as a rainbow.

Unable to change? Breathe **Fire**. Like a candle. Jump up and down until your heart starts pumping. Ask the Sun Grandfather, "How can I stop being so angry?" Listen. Keep aligning with the **Fire** and something will change.

Can't stop think-think-think-thinking? (Who can?) Calmly breathe. Put all of your willingness into every breath. Now you are aligning with the **Air** Elemental. Choose to remember out loud: *Intentional breath brings body and soul together faster than anything else.* Affirm that. Freely choose to know that and practice that. Freely choose to know that and practice that again and again. Our vast mental capabilities came into being through repetition. Utilize the **Air** Elemental positively and use words and thoughts to think what you really want now and continually. Don't forget to stand in the wind and appreciate all forms of weather. The **Air** Elemental is definitely smiling now.

Feeling sick? Are you unable to get even simple things done? Bring in the **Earth** Elemental. Get out in nature. This is the fun one. Now you have an excuse to camp or stand on a mountain, play with crystals, walk barefoot, dance—even if you don't know how to. Everybody can dance, they just have to demonstrate the appropriate willingness. Eat really good food. Drink strong herbal tea. While you are doing any of this, appreciate all of it minutely. Find every single thing that you love about being on the Earth. This changes everything regardless of what your defenses think or have to say about it. When you are ungrounded, you are trying too hard and doing too little. You have simply detoured too much of your body's energy into fighting the natural cycles of life. Stop. Ground with the Earth Mother Herself. The time and space you invest in this give you a boost of energy that gets every task done with time and energy to spare.

If you still don't know which Elemental to align with to balance you now, breathe with the **Ethers**. In the 3rd dimension, the **Ethers** are where **Earth**, **Fire**, **Water** and **Air** meet and integrate. They slip seamlessly into each other and that embrace is **Ethers**. Just breathe that. Understanding is not required in order to do it and be it. Call upon the **Ethers** for help. Meet your own guides there. Talk to your soul. You can say anything. In this space you are utterly known and still completely loved. Face yourself with all of the Elementals and awaken to embodying whole consciousness. That is you and the **Ethers** combined.

The above alignings, where you match the quality of your challenge to a similar quality in the corresponding Elemental, is the most immediate way to freely align yourself. We do it all day long. It is a habit of life. The more you repeat it, the more you make lifeforce available to you. Some meditations and visualizations tend to take you out of body. Aligning with the Elementals is a full body/senses experience. It interweaves you with all of the prove-able ways of life. So of course you *are* more alive. You have more gifts than you ever owned before and you are putting them right to use. When you do that, life SHOUTS, "Yes!" and gives you more. You use it and life makes more.

Remember in the **Water** Elemental example when we talked about how healing will be asked of us in many different forms and ways? It is the same with the Elementals. They offer us endless ways to align with them and therefore balance. After all, life is endless. Another immediate way to utilize the Elementals is to call upon a complementary Elemental to your situation. For instance, let's say you are really frustrated. So you want to calm that down. Breathing **Fire** sometimes just makes more **Fire**, more anger. A complementary Elemental could be the **Earth**. Walk around the block. Sit quietly at the park. Hang out with your dog. All of that **Fire** energy and anger can be channeled productively into the **Earth** Elemental. It gets you back into your body and reintroduces you to Earthy qualities like practicality, grounding, stamina. Grounding **Fire** takes anger and turns it into creativity. It happens so spontaneously that you might not notice it at first. Yet when you do ride its wave, note what grounding activities work the best for YOU and they will be habits turned into instincts. When you get frustrated you will immediately see yourself walking around the block, etc. Balancing with a complementary Elemental doesn't shew away what you don't like. It simply gives it a productive way to express itself. That is why the Elementals themselves constantly dance and change. They know that the nature of life is change and they reflect that. They do that inherently. When we align, we do the same. **We are changing Elementals.**

In our experience when you want to calm and re-channel an Elemental feeling, align with the corresponding non-symbiotic Elemental. In the above example we toned down and transformed sometimes destructive **Fire** with productive **Earth**. The same thing can ring true with **Air** and Water. If you can't stop talking, breathe **Water**. It spontaneously opens your heart. It listens. You listen. Likely your heart will tell you what you are so desperate to say that just isn't getting said. Usually talking too much points to an underlying emotion that hasn't found its way to the surface to be expressed. **Water** transforms excessive **Air**. Now everybody is breathing easier.

Another way of balancing with the Elementals is when you want to awaken and increase certain Elemental qualities. Let's say that the **Water** in the above example wants to be expressed more. One way to do this is to offer it the **Earth** Elemental. Now you are giving a home where those emotions are safe to be. When we feel safe and respected we spontaneously express our true natures in the moment. Instead of being inordinately shy, we speak up. We act upon what our heart wants. That is a love meeting between **Water** and **Earth**. To increase and expand upon one Elemental, bring in its symbiotic partner. Together they are no longer subject to 1+1=2. They are dancing <u>exponentially</u>. In the new math, 1+1 is whatever you want it to be. It = 10, 1000, or 33 million. They answer life according to the need and the desire.

How does **Ethers** fit in these balancings? Like the wild card it is, it is symbiotic with everything. When you don't know what to do, just go to the **Ethers**. Breathe with them, talk with them, feel them thoroughly. Now you know their nature: they are change and stillness, equally, simultaneously. Yes, you are right; they are both symbiotic and complementary to all of the other Elementals, according to whatever dances balance in the moment. Perfection. Ultimately it is all perfection, no matter how hard we try to escape it . . .

Practice . . .

We trust that you are aligning with the Elementals WHILE you are reading this. After all, the beauty of that aligning and balancing is that you can do it as you are doing everything/anything else. Whatever happens, **breathe** the Elemental that you want to increase (or its symbiotic partner); or breathe one that's non- symbiotic (to the one that you are experiencing the most right now) to calm down and heal with unconditional grace and ease. Personally, we like breathing **Water** while reading so that our heart is integrating the richness of what is being said, instead of just taking in words in our mind.

And of course it goes without saying that you may want to stop before anything that you want to truly focus on and align with the Elementals through at least one complete cycle: **Earth**; **Fire**; **Water**; **Air**; and **Ethers**. That way, you enter that activity as balanced as possible. As humans— especially fast-changing, evolving ones– we bounce in and out of balance so much all day long that we often don't know consciously if/when we are in balance or not. That's why it supports us automatically when we develop a regular ritual of aligning with the Elementals: It keeps us balanced; therefore we are more present, we can give and receive more than we imagined was possible.

As adults, we have habituated separateness from everything. And we are so accustomed to it, we don't even realize it most of the time. We keep reacting to the world from separation while trying to evolve to, and in, union (our true, natural state with our Spirits). Hence we need to be around as many beings/things/habits of union as possible so that we wake up that perspective within us and act upon that. We <u>can</u> (and ultimately do) choose union. It simply takes practice, like aligning with the Elementals and linking to our EBI's.

Another way to practice union is to be around children. They haven't learned to react to the world with as much separation yet. They inherently act from their EBI, still. Watch them closely. Learn. They are their EBI's spontaneously. When you absorb that, you automatically absorb your own EBI.

Our bodies inherently practice "entrainment." That means when we are around a higher frequency, our bodies stop their lower ones and attune themselves to the higher one. That's what happens to us when we open up to small children. Even though they may not be able to explain in words what their EBI is and how they link to it, their bodies are still **doing** it. Their bodies show our bodies how to do the Elemental dance. Just bring your willingness and do it.

Obviously, we encourage families to work with the Elementals together. It links everyone on core levels and automatically demonstrates how different EBI's work, play and learn together. When situations between people are painful and challenging, we can look to our EBI's— our innate link to healing and union— to balance us at the core, so that we can connect to each other with a bigger, freer perspective. It spontaneously takes the defensiveness off of the situation if we can stop relating to each other as victim/perpetrator (or whatever unhelpful, unconscious roles we are playing), and instead talk about the two EBI's and how they are learning to heal as best they can.

We have a story from a friend that illustrates this. She (Let's call her, Annie) was having problems connecting with her young daughter (Erin). No matter how much they talked over things, Erin felt more frustrated and more hopeless. Their conversations came to a standstill, so Annie, who already knew her EBI, asked her daughter, "Could we check and find out what your EBI is?" Erin who knew nothing about EBI's said, "Yes."

Annie is a calm, gentle Air/Earth. When Erin would blow up, Annie would go into repair mode and offer endless, patient solutions to keep Erin from feeling so angry. She truly was offering Erin the very best of what she had to give. Her Air likes to talk, to objectively mediate, while her Earth specializes in patient, practical solutions. In short, Annie was automatically giving Erin what she, Annie, likely would have wanted if the situations were reversed, yet all it did was piss off Erin even more.

We listened for Erin's EBI and it is Fire/Water. Yes! Of course, Erin is very emotional. Yes, she blows up because she feels everything so intensely that she needs, fast, powerful releases. When she explodes, she needs to give off steam. She's not asking for someone to explain life to her at the moment, she probably just wants them to back off and let her fireworks blaze away (and if Annie just gives Erin some space at that moment, Erin won't have to worry about Annie getting hurt in the explosion).

When you look at their EBI's, you can figure it out. Annie's EBI is not immediately emotional. She relies more on intellect and logic. So when she sees Erin blow up, Annie gets really stressed. Her instincts come to the fore and they tell her, "Who would want to feel that uncomfortable! Help her. You know how to do it. Get her calmed down and then tell her lots of ways to fix things. That's what she needs." So Annie does just that and pronto. And she does it with extra gentleness, so as not to rile Erin any further.

Erin's Fire/Water makes her quick, changeable, moody and empathic. When Annie has the audacity to TALK to her when Erin's screaming, she doesn't feel her mom's understanding, just her "wanting to fix things." For Erin, that's like saying, "It's not just the situation that's wrong, it's you. You must be really messed up to be so mad and to be so emotional all the time. Why can't you calm down and be more like me?"

Instead, Erin wants empathy; she probably wants somebody who can jump up and down in fury at injustices, too. That would make her feel like something was being immediately accomplished. It validates the very core of her being instantly. Now the steam's vented and she can smile again. Erin may or may not want to do anything else. She's not as concerned about the next logical thing to do, what's most important to her is that she released a lot of hard emotions pressing down on her. They're gone. She's ready to deal with life again.

From a purely Elemental standpoint, let's see how Annie's and Erin's EBI's combine. First of all, each has exactly the 2/4 physical Elementals (The physical Elementals are all the Elementals except Ethers.), that the other doesn't have: Air/Earth, Fire/Water. They don't share a common Elemental. At the core, they don't immediately share the same life view. When people get stressed, they go right to their EBI (usually subconsciously) and act instinctively from that. When Annie and Erin do that, they don't look at things the same way. They have a hard time understanding each other and they don't even know why: "I'm doing the best I can. Can't she see that? Can't she see that I'm right?" etc., etc.

Under happier circumstances, these EBI's will always teach other, because they do have different perspectives. When Annie opens her heart, Erin will meet her there. They will really feel each other. Annie might understand Erin in new ways, while Erin finally feels understood— accepted just for what she is in the moment, every moment.

Here comes the flip side: when Erin offers her objectivity and truly wants to learn from everything (translation: when she opens her mind), Annie rejoices, because she has libraries of information that she can share with her daughter. She's just been waiting for this moment. Now they can talk about anything and they both are learning. Annie is thrilled to share things that she knows will truly help her daughter over a lifetime.

Another thing happens when you combine Annie's and Erin's EBI's. They're also symbiotic. Annie has **Air** first and Erin has **Fire** first. Annie's **Air** fuels Erin's **Fire**. Her words incite Erin. They inspire her. They seem to really frustrate her. It goes on and on. **Air** and **Fire** go together so easily that they have a lot of energy to interacting. On a human level, that can mean whether or not they're getting along, they keep intersecting each other's path. Somehow they can't avoid each other. When you want to learn together and enjoy the pleasures of each other's company what could be better? When you have a lot of healing to do, it's still great to be activating that, but it feels pretty challenging.

Annie's and Erin's 2nd Elementals (**Earth** and **Water**, respectively) are symbiotic too. The way that they <u>act</u> upon their core beliefs fuels each other. Annie's **Earth** wants to wrap around Erin's formless, flowing water. She wants to protect her, to guide her, to teach her what she's learned that works in life. She wants Erin to be dependable and to mature gracefully. Erin on the other hand, brings imagination, love and easy-goingness to her mother's traditions. She gives them *feeling*, so that Annie doesn't just keep on responding to things in the same, old, dry way. She helps her mom to remember to **love** everything even when it's utterly illogical. Life IS more fun that way.

So now you see how EBI's can work in real life. It's simple. It helps you to bridge to others when you don't know how to do it. It takes away our need to be right in a conflict because we stop looking at the personalities clashing; we just let those go and start over and see how these EBI's CAN work together now. But getting back to real life, we want to tell you what happened with Annie and Erin. When Annie told Erin her EBI, the girl said, "I knew it. I just knew it." Both of them felt understanding when they knew both of their EBI's, "Oh, that's why you're like that." Erin stopped trying to get her mom emotional, because she now knows that's not really in Annie's nature. Probably always, Annie's going to react differently than that. And that's okay with Erin. Her mom's not **trying** to annoy Erin when Erin's dramatic, she just uses that energy in another way and always will. It's okay, that's just her mom. They both have found new ways of accepting each other and that released a lot of struggle from their relationship, overnight. It is a blessing.

As we said earlier, it's glorious when adults can be around youngsters. Kids are more spontaneous with their true natures. They walk and talk their EBI's. If the rest of us simply watch, we learn. We learn how the Elementals dance and therefore how to wake up our true nature. We're here to be ourselves! Even when it's not fun, it satisfies us. It heals us. It connects us to life at the source where we can endlessly fuel our real destinies.

Planetary Elemental Grids

The only beings on the Earth that have Elemental Birth Imprints are humans, because they are the only ones whom upon birth forget themselves. On a certain, real-world level, we lose our Spirits and enter the world of separation where we instinctively focus our energies on survival alone. Happiness, creativity, evolution go right out of our minds upon our first breath outside of our mother. It's all life or death and we end up focusing on death. So how do we link back to that in utero time where we still breathed water and union? Well, one way is to be around children and let our bodies entrain to theirs because they act out from their EBI's more readily. Not only is that a good idea, it's fun. It's pure joy to dance with them and the Elementals. Still, we have found another way that really helps us to ground the Elementals into our bodies and lives.

We love traveling around the world doing EBI workshops. It's fantastic. It bonds us with people at the core and we learn volumes. One of the things we noticed in Japan, for instance, was that we saw a high percentage of symbiotic EBI's. We asked our Spirit Grandmother why this was and she told us something unexpected. She said that while two-leggeds are the only ones on the planet who have EBI's, the Earth Mother is so simultaneously synchronized with the Elementals and humans that she bridges between them uniquely and generously, on our behalf. While she doesn't have an EBI per se, she does allow us to feel Her body in Elemental Grids. Translation: Different countries or regions of the Earth can possess EBI's for people who want to be guided that way.

As it turns out, for us Japan has an **Earth/Water** Grid. As goes the Earth, so goes the humans. No wonder so many people there had symbiotic imprints. Their bodies and souls were naturally reflecting the Elemental Grid of where they were born. The Elementals imprint us and so does the Earth. Of course.

We could see and feel that **Earth/Water** commonalities in our Japanese friends. Most of them were naturally grounded and calm, even under stress. Also, they seem to be very emotional and extremely respectful of everyone's emotions.

This also explained to us why our Spirits call to us to actually put our feet on different parts of the Earth, even when it seemed to make no immediate sense. Once there, we realized that those Elemental Grids were imprinting us. They give us their Elemental nature to absorb so that we can instantaneously evolve (which is why we feel we are here on the Earth now). During our first trip to Japan, we felt that we had somehow come home. We loved how quiet it was, even in the Tokyo airport. Most of all, we deeply appreciated how respectful these strangers were with us and each other. The bowing says it all.

We were absorbing new levels of **Earth/Water** immediately.

That got us to listening to other regions of the Earth for their EBI's:
(Note: There are no percentages of the Elementals with Earth EBI's, though the first Elemental is the strongest and so on, down from there)

Afghanistan- **Fire/Earth**
Albania- **Water/Air**
Algeria- **Air/Fire**
American Samoa- **Water/Fire**
Andorra- **Earth/Fire**
Angola- **Fire**
Anguilla- **Air/Water**
Antarctica & outlying islands- **Air**
Antigua- **Earth/Water**
Arctic- **Earth**
Argentina- **Fire/Earth**
Armenia- **Earth/Fire**
Aruba- **Water/Fire**
Ascension Islands- **Air/Water**
Australia & outlying islands- **Water/Fire**
Austria- **Air/Water**
Azerbaijan- **Air/Earth**
Bahamas- **Water with an Etheric Overlay**
Bahrain- **Fire/Water**
Bangladesh- **Earth/Air**
Barbados- **Air/Water**
Belarus- **Earth**
Belgium- **Air/Water**
Belize- **Water/Earth**

Benin- **Earth/Fire**
Bermuda- **Water**
Bhutan- **Air/Fire**
Bolivia- **Air/Earth**
Bosnia & Herzegovina- **Air/Water**
Botswana- **Earth/Water**
Bouvet Island- **Fire/Earth**
Brazil- **Earth/Fire**
British Indian Ocean Territory- **Air/Water**
Brunei- **Earth/Water**
Bulgaria- **Earth**
Burkina Faso- **Earth/Air**
Burundi- **Fire/Earth**
Cambodia- **Air/Fire**
Cameroon- **Air/Water**
Canada & outlying islands- **Air/Earth**
Cape Verde- **Water**
Cayman Islands- **Fire/Water**
Central African Republic- **Earth/Air**
Chad- **Earth/Air**
Chile- **Water/Fire**
China- **Water/Air**
Christmas Island- **Air/Earth**
Cocos Island- **Water**

Comoros- **Water/Air**
Congo- **Water/Earth**
Costa Rica- **Fire/Water**
Croatia- **Air/Water**
Cuba- **Earth/Fire**
Cyprus- **Fire/Water**
Czech Republic- **Earth/Air**
Denmark- **Earth/Water**
Djibouti- **Fire/Water**
Dominica- **Water**
Dominican Republic- **Water/Air**
Earth- **Water/Earth**
East Timor- **Air**
Ecuador- **Water/Air/Fire**
Egypt- **Air/Fire, Ethers underpinning**
El Salvador- **Fire**
Equatorial Guinea- **Fire/Earth**
Eritrea- **Water/Air**
Estonia- **Water/Air**
Ethiopia- **Earth/Air**
Falkland Islands- **Air**
Faroe Islands- **Air/Air**
Fiji- **Water/Earth**
Finland- **Water/Air**

– 94 –

France- **Earth/Fire**

French Guiana- **Fire**

French Metropolitan- **Fire/Water**

French Polynesia- **Water/Earth**

French Southern Territories- **Fire/Earth**

Gabon- **Air/Fire**

Gambia- **Air/Water**

Georgia- **Water/Air**

Germany- **Air/Water**

Ghana- **Water/Air**

Gibraltar- **Fire/Water**

Great Britain- **Earth/Air**

Greece- **Fire**

Greenland & outlying islands- **Earth**

Grenada- **Air/Water**

Guadeloupe- **Water**

Guam- Water/**Earth**

Guatemala- **Fire/Water**

Guernsey- **Air/Water**

Guinea- **Fire**

Guinea-Bissau- **Water/Earth**

Guyana- **Fire/Earth**

Haiti- **Earth/Fire**

Heard & McDonald Islands- **Fire**

Holy Sea- **Air/Water**

Honduras- **Earth/Water**

Hong Kong- **Fire/Water**

Hungary- **Earth/Water**

Iceland & outlying islands- **Water/Air**

India- **Ethers/Air**

Indonesia & outlying islands- **Water/Earth**

Iran- **Fire/Fire**

Iraq- **Fire/Earth**

Ireland- **Water**

Isle of Man- **Water/Earth**

Israel- **Fire/Earth**

Italy- **Fire/Air**

Jamaica- **Earth/Water/Air**

Japan- **Earth/Water**

Jersey- **Air/Earth**

Jordan- **Fire/Fire/Water**

Kazakhstan- **Air/Water**

Kenya- **Air/Air**

Kiribati- **Water/Earth**

Korea, North- **Fire/Air**

Korea, South- **Fire/Earth**

Kosovo- **Fire/Water**

Kuwait- **Water/Air**

Kyrgyzstan- **Air/Earth**

Laos- **Earth/Fire**

Latvia- **Air/Fire**

Lebanon- **Fire/Earth**

Lesotho- **Earth/Air**

Liberia- **Water/Air**

Libya- **Fire**

Liechtenstein- **Air/Earth**

Lithuania- **Earth**

Luxembourg- **Water/Air**

Macau- **Water/Earth**

Macedonia- **Earth/Air**

Madagascar- **Water/Earth**

Malawi- **Air/Earth**

Malaysia- **Water/Fire**

Maldives- **Water/Air**

Mali- **Water/Air**

Malta- **Water/Earth**

Marshall Islands- **Water/Fire**

Martinique- **Fire/Air**

Mauritania- **Water/Earth**

Mauritius- **Water**

Mayotte- **Earth/Fire**

Mexico- **Water/Fire**

Micronesia- **Fire/Water**

Moldova- **Fire/Earth**

Monaco- **Air/Fire**

Mongolia- **Air/Water**

Montenegro- **Air/Earth**

Montserrat- **Water/Earth**

Morocco- **Fire/Earth**
Mozambique- **Water/Fire**
Myanmar- **Water/Fire**
Namibia- **Earth/Fire**
Nauru- **Water/Earth**
Nepal- **Ethers/Earth**
Netherlands- **Air/Water**
Netherlands Antilles- **Water/Air**
New Caledonia- **Fire/Water**
New Zealand- **Earth/Fire**
Nicaragua- **Fire/Air**
Niger- **Air**
Niue- **Earth/Fire**
Norfolk Island- **Fire/Air**
Northern Mariana Islands- **Water/Air**
Norway- **Air/Earth**
Oman- **Air/Fire**
Pakistan- **Fire/Ethers**
Palau- **Fire/Earth**
Palestinian National Authority- **Fire/Water**
Panama- **Water/Earth**
Papua New Guinea- **Fire/Earth**
Paraguay- **Fire/Water**
Peru- **Air/Fire**
Philippines- **Water**
Pitcairn Islands- **Fire/Water**

Poland- **Water/Earth**
Portugal- **Fire/Earth**
Puerto Rico- **Water/Fire**
Qatar- **Fire**
Romania- **Earth/Water**
Russia- **Water/Water**
Rwanda- **Water/Fire**
Saint Kitts and Nevis- **Water**
Saint Lucia- **Water/Fire**
Saint Vincent and Grenadines- **Air/Water**
Samoa- **Water/Fire**
San Marino- **Air/Fire**
Sao Tome and Principe- **Earth/Fire**
Saudi Arabia- **Fire/Earth**
Senegal- **Earth/Water**
Serbia- Air/Water
Seychelles- **Fire/Earth**
Sierra Leone- **Fire/Earth**
Singapore- **Air/Fire**
Slovakia- **Earth/Air**
Solomon Islands- **Earth/Fire**
Slovenia- **Water/Air**
Somalia- **Water/Fire**
South Africa- **Air/Water**
South Georgia and South Sandwich Islands- **Earth**
South Sudan- **Earth/Fire**

Spain- **Fire/Water**
Sri Lanka- **Water/Earth**
St Helena- **Fire**
St Pierre and Miquelon- **Water/Air**
Sudan- **Fire**
Suriname- **Water/Fire**
Svalbard and Jan Mayen Islands- **Air/Water**
Swaziland- **Earth/Fire**
Sweden- **Air/Water/Earth**
Switzerland- **Air/Fire**
Syria- **Fire/Air**
Taiwan- **Water/Fire**
Tajikistan- **Air**
Tanzania- **Air/Water**
Thailand- **Water/Earth**
Tibet- **Ethers/Air**
Togo- **Water/Air**
Tokelau- **Water**
Tonga- **Earth/Air**
Trinidad & Tobago- **Earth/Water**
Tunisia- **Water/Fire**
Turkey- **Air/Water**
Turkmenistan- **Earth**
Turks and Caicos Islands- **Earth/Water**
Tuvalu- **Air/Water**
Uganda- **Air**

Ukraine- **Earth/Air**	Vanuatu- **Fire/Earth**	Wallis and Futuna- **Water/Earth**
United Arab Emirates- **Fire/Water**	Vatican City- **Water**	Western Sahara- **Air/Earth**
United Kingdom- **Air/Water**	Venezuela- **Water/Fire**	Yemen- **Fire**
USA & outlying islands- **Air/Fire/Water**	Vietnam- **Water/Air**	Zaire- **Earth/Fire/Water**
Uruguay- **Air/Water**	Virgin Islands, British- **Water/Earth**	Zambia- **Earth**
Uzbekistan- **Air/Water**	Virgin Islands, US- **Water/Air**	Zimbabwe- **Air/Earth**

Combine your EBI with the different areas of the Earth and you will see what gifts you can give and receive from that area. You don't have to go there physically to do it. Study that region and see what things about it speak to you intuitively. Meditate with their Elementals and ask them to download you with their wisdom.

In our travels, we found ourselves downloaded with powerful sensations and feelings from the Elementals. This helps us to manifest with the flow of what's happening around us and it increases our listening. Our bodies come alive with senses of other dimensions and other ways of life.

For all of us, aligning our EBI with the area that we live in empowers us. So many humans fight the Earth and don't even know it (survival instincts). When you touch the Elemental heart of your home, you feel union. You ground into it. Your body likes matching that vibration. Literally you are in the flow of all things and vice versa. Deep appreciation guides your days.

Conception Imprints

There's one more thing that integrates the EBI for us: Conception Imprints. We didn't want to mention them until the very end of the book because learning and practicing your EBI is the most empowering ritual of union that we know of now. We encourage you to focus on the EBI over the Conception Imprint whenever possible.

Now that we established that, let's talk Conception Imprints. When we were conceived, our parents' bodies were surfing very powerful Elemental waves and at the exact peak of this activity, we were conceived. In that moment, one Elemental imprints us. It represents the Elemental energy gift that came to us from our parents. It starts us off and we grow from that, breeding our own uniqueness.

Knowing your CI helps you to know your parents (and ultimately all humans) at the core. Whatever they were feeling, being and acting upon in conceiving you encourages you to connect with them. This empowers you to know yourself and all of life more readily. Sometimes when you reach an impasse in healing and evolving, knowing your CI gives you a boost. It can be an unexpected "Aha!" when you don't know where else to turn.

The other primary way to utilize your CI is to combine it with your EBI. See how that shakes things up. It may explain how certain deep tendencies began. Once you are at the core, anything can happen. And with a little open-hearted willingness, CI's will show you a natural, beautiful continuum of life that makes you humbly honor your place within it.

Earth Conception Imprint

Mostly you know how to ground because at conception your parents were aware of their bodies and their senses. They wanted to be present with each other and feel the strength of that union. They were easy to please; they wanted to be satisfied with the way life was/is. This imprinted you with a usually unshakeable sense of yourself, a certain security that no one can take away.

Fire Conception Imprint

Deep down you know how to tap a river of creativity if you need it, because your parents gifted you that. In conceiving you, they set aside (consciously or subconsciously) their own desires and selves for something bigger. What brought them together was seeing how life could be and they wanted as big a change as they could. Maybe something inspired them and opened them up to newness. Because of this you truthfully feel like everything will always get better.

Water Conception Imprint

You innately feel everything to some degree, no matter what your EBI is. Some profound emotions sparked your parents when you were conceived. Maybe they didn't fully realize it or understand it, but they followed its flow without much question. They were learning trust and so are you—different lessons, the same issue.

Air Conception Imprint

Many different things could have been happening when you were conceived. This CI suggests that your parents were thinking about a lot. Some of it may have been worries, but mostly they were trying very hard to learn, to understand. That's how they came together and that's what they imparted to you. When you get really stressed, you really want to understand life so that you can help things to improve.

Ethers Conception Imprint

There were many energies present when you were conceived. Your parents were unusually tuned into their Spirits and felt profoundly guided by that even if they didn't understand. Sometimes this means that they may have been remembering family members that had already passed on. People with this CI tend to be more aware of consciousness and aspire to a more multi-dimensional life.

Afterwords

Thus ends this book, but certainly not the adventure. We wrote this book like we do all things, listening to the Elementals. So we wrote this while we were (and are) still actively, gratefully learning about EBI's. Before writing this book, most people would have done a lot of research and tested it out extensively to understand all the parameters and then, after a long time, they would write the book. We understand that. We didn't do that.

It's true that we lived and breathed the EBI's for years. We didn't study them; we wore ours into every situation 24/7. EBI's were (and are) so exciting, so timely and so elegantly *simple,* we had to take them out into the world as soon as possible. Immediately after that, it became gloriously clear that EBI's touched people's lives deeply. They change everything spontaneously and forever. We are so filled with awe, we consciously choose to learn and share these miraculous gifts from our Spirits both simultaneously and always.

The learning and sharing are growing exponentially. You are, now, part of a great and grand evolving that is teaching us all what we most profoundly need to know and to be, right in this exact moment. The awareness of the existence of EBI's landed upon us now because we need them, now, when we are outgrowing our previous rules/measurements/understanding. The Earth is changing in a blink and we must join Her with equally new and utterly honoring ways of life; otherwise we will not survive and thrive and meet our true, Spirit-filled destinies. This is why simple, immediate, profound EBI's have entered our awareness.

Join them. Listen. Watch. Need more guidance? Watch how the Elementals move in nature, that will immediately tell you about your nature/our nature. Still want more? Of course you do. Dance with them and love every step.

Welcome to the Elemental Birth Imprint DECK

Yes, we JUMPED on Elemental Birth Imprints from the moment that our Spiritual Grandmother presented them to us! They were so timely, and so perfect, we couldn't wait to share them with everyone—with **you**.

Once we did that, kind folks said, "Hey! I can't keep all this straight . . . what do you mean I got **Water** in my **Fire**?" and most of all, "**When** are you going to write the BOOK on EBI's!"

Thanks everybody for asking that. Your lovely insistence helped launch the BOOK that you are reading and aligning with right now. But while we were in the process of still finishing this, we found we had to quickly write the most basic information that we could about as many EBI's possible. So we made a card DECK of basic EBI's and got that to some of you who were **jumping** on that information right away, and then we were also able to begin using the DECK in our EBI workshops as well.

Now that the BOOK is here, we are also including that sweet, succinct information from the DECK here, for easy, spontaneous reference. When life is so crazy you want to scream (Go for it!), grab this part of the BOOK and in a few sentences, you can and will align with your perfect, glorious Elemental Birth Imprint. Everything will change: You will join with life in honor and magnificence, again.

So here's how you can read/align with any EBI card. First of all, it starts off with just a sentence or two that sums up the general mission of everyone with that Imprint. It answers the ever important, "Why am I here really?" Getting that response deeply and continually encourages you to always go to the biggest, most generous, utterly loving, life-enhancing perspective possible. Once there, you will find your true priorities. Talk about making life a simple joy . . .

Then, the card lists "Potential Inhibitors"—a few phrases that display possible qualities you might have that could challenge you on your way to being your most magnificent self. Go ahead and cringe when you read these—everybody does—just get that judgment out of your system so you can really, truly befriend the "Potential Inhibitors." Why? It's because while we all **love** hearing our talents— what makes us look bright and shiny to ourselves and to the world—knowing our challenges well enough to change them, always, in all ways, strengthens us beyond anything else.

Grandmother ever says to us, "Whatever are your strengths are your weaknesses and whatever are your weaknesses are your strengths—just the same." She explains that life gives us all gifts and challenges and *what we do with them* determines whether they will manifest ultimately as gifts, or challenges, in our reality. Energy is just energy; it doesn't judge what we do with it.

So, yes, we **focus** on our gifts; we choose to come from our positive foundation in every breath, every day, because we adore making and sharing miracles. We depend on them for our very reality and we love that! It is so magnificent. And to get there, we receive every single gift AND challenge given to us and we unconditionally accept the courage and the inspiration they offer us. They are all gifts and we USE them. When we completely love and appreciate the lifeforce they offer us, they turn into rocket fuel for spectacular realities. Once we stop using up all our energy to hate them, we have endless lifeforce to make magic. Or as Tohmas says, "I post my Potential Inhibitors right next to my desk in BIG letters so I can be reminded of them constantly instead of having to draw dramas to me as reflections in order to be aware and to evolve!"

Try it. For just this moment, accept your Potential Inhibitors. How does it feel? Whatever you do, try not to take it personally, and just ask the Potential Inhibitors, "What's your gift for me? What can I do for you? How can we heal?"

The Potential Inhibitors, like your EBI, already know you, and they never judge you or anything, for that matter. They look you right in the eye and trust you with the truth, "Maybe this is you on a hard day. Maybe not, but check it out. Somewhere, some day it will teach you something glorious . . . *Lean* into it."

Have you posted yours yet?

The final category on each EBI card is "Potential Resources." Everybody immediately loves these— even when they pretend otherwise— because they show off your talents. It affirms that you are the spectacular, unique genius that your heart has been saying forever. And it's right. This proves it.

JUMP on your "Potential Resources." They literally live, at-the-ready, to align with your positive foundation, now. Now. No extra time needed to transmute their qualities into something life enhancing and enchanting, they are already there.

Since we know there are challenges and gifts to everything, and we know already what the immediate gifts are in the "Potential Resources," what are the **challenges?** All of us are born with immediate, easy talents/gifts that show up so beautifully. And we admire their inherent grace so much sometimes we forget to use them. And then they just disappear from lack of use, like un-exercised muscles, which turn to flab. Now we have "talents" that not only aren't serving us, they take from our potentials.

"Whatever are your strengths are your weaknesses and whatever are your weaknesses are your strengths. What you DO with that focus and abundance of energy is what turns them into strengths or weaknesses." What you do with your "Potential Inhibitors" or "Potential Resources" is what defines them and you. Simple. They are called "Potentials," for a reason . . .

This DECK also includes the five possible **Conception Imprints**. These cards start summarizing the spectrum of beingness and doing-ness that you can embody in this life from the energies of your conception. Then it progresses to the "Challenges from Your Family," and the "Gifts from Your Family." Yeehaaawww! Objectively befriending these challenges and gifts makes you stand like your own tree: massive roots, gorgeous trunk and branches, and while you're right next to the whole forest, you're just perfectly, individually YOU. There isn't another thing you really need that you can't attract for yourself.

Put your EBI and CI together. Does it look like you? Would you like to change it? *How?* Love those qualities and something wonderful happens all the time.

Welcome to your real life . . .

Elemental Birth Imprint Deck

– Earth –

You are here to embody.
Your learning and talent is to experience everything
of the Earth plane and the Earth Mother,
especially limits and structures.

Potential Inhibitors: *Too fixed; Stubborn; Too bound to gravity and authority.*
Potential Resources: *Innately connected to all things; Sense of profound belonging; Deep, healthy self-esteem; Reverence for all.*

– Air –

You are here
to explore mental energy.
Your challenges and talents are:
curiosity, quickness and/or scatteredness
and all forms of communication and definitions.

Potential Inhibitors: *Easily distracted; Unable to prioritize; Too much multi-tasking; Not breathing fully.*
Potential Resources: *Utilizes breath as prana; Learns easily and quickly; Curious and bold adventurer.*

– Fire –

You are here
to initiate lifeforce and creativity.
Your challenges and gifts are:
spontaneity, flashes of intuition, the gut emotions/passions
and the most profound changes possible.

Potential Inhibitors: *Anger; Impatient; Demanding; Willful; Sexual issues.*
Potential Resources: *Passionate; Wildly creative; Changes easily, spontaneously and profoundly.*

– Water –

You are here
to feel all of life.
Your talents and challenges
are all emotions, empathy, telepathy, and compassion.

Potential Inhibitors: *Introverted; Closed heart; Opinionated; Isolated.*
Potential Resources: *Understands all of life; Immediate penetrating wisdom; Allowability; Flowing.*

– Ethers –

Ethers are the great mysteries
and the Spirit that moves in all things.
You are here to express consciousness in all acts, thoughts and feelings.

Potential Inhibitors: *Inability to integrate anything; Depression; Uselessness.*
Potential Resources: *All pervasive presence; Timeless knowingness; Trust; Faith; Easily connects to guides.*

– Earth/Earth –

Welcome to planet Earth!
You belong here, even when you think otherwise.
Your job is to find every way to connect
to every part of the Earth experience with stability,
practicality and simple acceptance.
Above all, be in your body and care for it.

Potential Inhibitors: *Ungrounded; Inability to focus or manifest; No stamina, discipline or perseverance.*
Potential Resources: *Can manifest anything; Dependable; Committed; Respond-able.*

– Air/Air –

You are here to experience
the openness and the limits of the mind.
You will learn continually throughout all of your life.

Potential Inhibitors: *Obsession; Defensive; Stuck in unhelpful/unhealthy habits; Unconscious.*
Potential Resources: *Ease with exploring anything, anytime, anyplace; Breathes deeply and well.*

– Fire/Fire –

You are here to experience passion,
inspiration and power.
You will vacillate between
evolving constantly and being afraid to change anything.

Potential Inhibitors: *Over-powering; Domineering; Inability to adjust to anyone else or other ways.*
Potential Resources: *Constantly evolving; Daring; Instinctual; Trusts deep impulses.*

– Water/Water –

You are here to feel yourself and all of life.
Every moment offers you the chance
to open or close your heart,
over and over again.

Potential Inhibitors: *Overly subjective; Inability to learn; Closed-down senses; Unrealistic.*
Potential Resources: *Identifies with anybody and anything; Surrenders to the divine order; Innately gracious and graceful.*

– Ethers/Ethers –

You are here to embody Spirit.
You walk in this world
with great or non-existent purpose.

Potential Inhibitors: *Inability to relate to life; Profoundly ungrounded; Inability to digest or integrate.*
Potential Resources: *Inexplicable inspiration; Humility; Tangibly connected to many dimensions simultaneously.*

– Earth/Air –

You are here to bring order and truth to manifestations.
Limits and unlimitedness will find you
in your breath and in your body.

Potential Inhibitors: *Unrooted; Living in your own world; Obsessed with rules and what can't be done.*
Potential Resources: *Health; Longevity; Acting upon your truth.*

– Earth/Fire –

You are here to imbue inspiration into everyday life.
You will lead or follow grand visions.

Potential Inhibitors: *Miserly; Bossy; Contrary; Unable to initiate.*
Potential Resources: *Offers magic to the mundane; Optimistic; Cosmic cheerleader.*

– Earth/Water –

You are here
to feel all things
in all experiences.
You will innately recognize
the flow and rhythms of nature.

Potential Inhibitors: *Heaviness; Inability to move or change; Powerless.*
Potential Resources: *Works/Plays in balance; Follows hunches well; Manifests dreams.*

– Earth/Ethers –

You are here
to unite Heaven and Earth.
Life invites you
to affirm the divine order in all things.

Potential Inhibitors: *Finds no purpose for life; Denial; Lives in fantasy.*
Potential Resources: *Everything is a meditation in Union with all innately; Understands what is beneath the surface.*

– Fire/Earth –

You are here to experience the underlying joy in every single thing.
You celebrate who and what you are.

Potential Inhibitors: *Overly authoritative; Irresponsible; Unable to commit; Inability to choose.*
Potential Resources: *Always makes things happen; Creates what was impossible before; Enlivens old traditions.*

– Fire/Air –

You are here to experience a common utopia.
You will find friends in every place.

Potential Inhibitors: *Afraid of intimacy; Inability to deal with details; Insatiable; Restless.*
Potential Resources: *Fantastic orator; Deals with groups beautifully; Excellent mediator.*

– Fire/ Water –

You
are here
to experience
every emotion.
Your heart is your guide.

Potential Inhibitors: *Inability to act; Self obsessed; Grandiose; Unable to release old patterns.*
Potential Resources: *Superb explorer; Profoundly present with people in the most extreme circumstances; Easily and continually intuits the underlying feelings and emotions.*

– Fire/Ethers –

You are here to experience transcendence.
You will travel in many worlds.

Potential Inhibitors: *Over-estimates abilities; Mistakes ego for divine guidance; Intolerant.*
Potential Resources: *Magnificent guide; Natural medium; Creates new traditions and new systems.*

– Water/Earth –

You are here to experience
the equal consciousness
of all beings upon the Earth.
Your presence brings reverence to all moments.

Potential Inhibitors: *Insulated; Fearful; Always needs things a certain way.*
Potential Resources: *Superb attention; Profound empathy; Defends vulnerable beings; Uses possessions and resources efficiently.*

– Water/Air –

You are here to experience
sharing and communicating feelings.
You will find friends at every level and in every place.

Potential Inhibitors: *Boredom; Inexpressive; Lonely.*
Potential Resources: *Versatile; Good left/right brain integration; Intuitive and logical.*

– Water/Fire –

You are here to experience
sharing your heart with the world at large.
Life will be both quiet and adventurous.

Potential Inhibitors: *Extremes of emotions; Volatile; Lack of perspective.*
Potential Resources: *Passionate; Good motivator; Leader in a crisis.*

– Water/Ethers –

You are here to experience
everything possible
on the Earth.
Innately,
you
give and receive
much love.

Potential Inhibitors: *Overly delusional; Poor boundaries; Lack of clarity; Incoherent.*
Potential Resources: *Inspired; Graciously supportive; Able to silently be present with anybody/anything.*

– Air/Earth –

You are here
to experience the practicality of harmony.
You give voice to all parts of the Earth.

Potential Inhibitors: *Indecisiveness; Acting w/o consideration; Unreliability.*
Potential Resources: *Knows how to utilize what is at hand; Recognizes hidden potentials; Excellent teacher.*

– Air/Fire –

You are here to experience
sharing visions and possibilities.
You constantly learn how to think anew.

Potential Inhibitors: *Too hasty; Finishes nothing; Waits for everyone else to manifest for them.*
Potential Resources: *Visionary; Genius; Can teach themselves anything; Dynamic.*

– Air/Water –

You are here to join reason and faith.
You bridge tradition with the new Earth paradigm.

Potential Inhibitors: *Vacillates between extremes; Unbalanced; Sneaky.*
Potential Resources: *Both objective and subjective; Understands anything; Reaches into the unknown and creates new tools for manifestation.*

– Air/Ethers –

You are here to experience
the known and the unknown simultaneously.
You can live your ideals.

Potential Inhibitors: *Naive; Vulnerable; Addictive; Escapist.*
Potential Resources: *Good traveler; Relates to any kind of person/experience; Thrives on the unknown; Excellent mediator.*

– Ethers/Earth –

You are here to experience
the difference between surviving and thriving.

Potential Inhibitors: *Accident prone; Melodramatic; Depressed.*
Potential Resources: *Disciplined; Ethical; Leader.*

– Ethers/Air –

You are here to experience every dimension of learning.
All things spark your interest.

Potential Inhibitors: *Unable to embody; Lack of priorities and values; Inconsistent.*
Potential Resources: *Profound imagination; Able to visualize clearly in 3 dimensions; Unique.*

– Ethers/Fire –

You are here to experience life on the edge.
Over time, no one will recognize you from your past.

Potential Inhibitors: *Fool-hardy; Driven; Proselytizing.*
Potential Resources: *Warm; Congenial; Able to bridge to many people simultaneously.*

– Ethers/Water –

You are here
to experience the unknown.
Your life is your own.

Potential Inhibitors: *Shy; Obsessive/Compulsive; Fearful; Overly focused on security.*
Potential Resources: *Self-sufficient; Homebody; Profoundly intimate.*

Elemental Conception Imprints

– Earth –

You are here to experience every practical reality.
Left to your own devices, you will find a way to overcome anything.

Challenges from your family: *Struggle; Competition; Overly ambitious.*
Gifts from your family: *Values; Efficiency; Patience.*

– Air –

You are here to communicate about life.
You will observe and learn.

Challenges from your family: *Too attached to unrealistic dreams; Impractical; Overly talkative.*
Gifts from your family: *Excellent balance; Diplomatic; Good teacher.*

– Fire –

You are here to experience passion.
You go from moment to moment seeking thrills and joy.

Challenges from your family: *Greedy; Lustful; Possessive.*
Gifts from your family: *Confident; Trusting; Able to take big risks successfully.*

– Water –

You are here to experience the feelings beneath the surface.
You love to love.

Challenges from your family: *Confused; Unclear; Nonassertive.*
Gifts from your family: *Chameleon-like; Surrenders gracefully; Focuses upon the needs of others easily.*

– Ethers –

You
are here
to experience.

Challenges from your family: *Inability to manifest desires; Lack of motivation; Not sympathetic.*
Gifts from your family: *Always able to find divine order; Passionate about true destiny; Able to transform any situation.*

Glossary

Note: In sharing the wisdom and ways that our life has gloriously gifted us, we use a lot of the same terms repeatedly . . . because our Spirits repeat them constantly with us, too. They are important. As they say to us, "Repetition is not necessarily redundant." Apparently we NEED to hear some things continually to truly learn and to reinforce that magic into this reality.

So we are briefly defining those terms for you, here, direct from our own experience of joining with the Elementals and our Spirits. If you, too, need to repeat them to evolve as you truly choose, here they are: simple, immediate, ready!

Keep repeating them and then evolve their meanings through your own experiences, through your own aligning and union with the Elementals. Then write your own Glossary and let the magic begin . . .

Aligning with the Elementals— *Through breath and conscious intent, we align the elements in our bodies (Earth/Fire/Water/Air/Ethers) with the Elementals (see "Elementals" below) in nature, to be in loving union with all of life upon the Earth Mother.*

BOOK— *We refer to this book as a "BOOK," so that we are always honoring its Spirit and the consciousness within it that is speaking, energetically, to each of us in exactly the way we need it and not just as the words-by-themselves portray. Yipppeeee!!!*

Cracks in your Shield— *These are the unresolved, unloved hurts that we humans store in our bodies and our beings until we are capable of healing them. Once healed, those cracks smooth over and they leave us to become new energy and magnificent, new life.*

Conception Imprint (CI)— *At the precise moment of our conception the Elementals (see "Elementals" below) imprint us with the qualities and energies of one of the elements: Earth/Fire/Water/Air/Ethers.*

Devic— *A Spirit of Nature, like the Spirit that naturally, happily resides in an animal, plant, mineral or weather, etc. Look for them!*

Elemental Birth Imprint (EBI)— *Just before we leave our mother's womb the Elementals (see "Elementals" below) imprint us with a combination of their energies that will subconsciously and/or consciously remind us of who we were before we learned to feel separate from: love, life, and our souls. This is pre-personality and happens while we still have a conscious link to Spirit/Union in the water element in the womb.*

Elementals— *The Devic Spirits within the elements of Earth/Fire/Water/Air/Ethers. Every moment they move in various patterns and concentrations of energy to form all matter (We are all made up of some combination of the elements.) and to balance all our energies on the Earth Mother moment-to-moment.*

Ethers— *The inherent consciousness and Spirit in everyone and everything that we celebrate abundantly.*

Evolution— *Each of us is born with the potential for complete enlightenment, where our body and soul—all that we are—come together and act in unconditional love and acceptance. The process of going from birth, through the illusion of being separate from our souls, to remembering and knowing that we are in loving union with all of life is evolution.*

Free Will— *We feel that on the soul level where everything unconditionally loves, we are all free will beings. Each of our souls freely chooses to come here to planet Earth to embody Spirit, even (and specifically) through experiencing seeming separation from our Spirit.*

Grandmother Sweet Shield— *Our Spiritual Grandmother who joins us across dimensions to talk with us, to witness our lives without judgment and to guide us as we accept and choose. She taught us about the Elementals and about how to align with them and about Elemental Birth Imprints and Conception Imprints.*

Healing— *This is when we completely open our hearts and unconditionally feel everything and then release it all to love. No one can do this for us. That's why even though others can help facilitate our healthy processes, only we can heal ourselves. For us, there really is no "healed" only living in a forever "healing" process.*

Healing your Shield— *Before a human incarnates on the Earth, their soul chooses how and when they will land here. As they are coalescing into form/body, some of their Spirit remains in the Ethers—unformed—and forever stays with that human and its body. We call this energy field, our Shield. Once we experience seeming separation from our Spirit and the coinciding, myriads of hurt, this cracks our Shield. As evolving humans, we choose to unconditionally love/embrace/release those hurts and this is "healing your Shield."*

Incarnation— *This is when your soul freely chooses to come to the Earth Mother and embodies for a lifetime of learning and healing.*

Listening— *This is when we open up our hearts to their fullest, unlimited potential and then we stay there long enough to feel all other respectful forms of life and hear their stories—potentially first and foremost as a witness without filters.*

Separation— *At the moment of birth, we feel like we are ejected out of our mother's womb into an unfriendly, unknown world, where we are completely separate—on some level—from everybody, everything, even our own Spirit.*

Spiritfamilies— *Whenever a soul is brave and unconditional enough to incarnate upon the Earth Mother, utterly loving families/guides from other realms stay with this human and support him/her unconditionally.*

Union— *At the core of our beings, we are love and consciousness and we are part of everything and everybody in the present moment.*

2-leggeds— *Humans—we are animals, like a lot of others. We simply are the 2-legged variety.*

About us

We're often silent hermits who live and work off-the-grid on the side of a mountain in the SW desert of the US. Even though we travel a lot (and adore it!) we return back to the land that named itself, Gandarvas, and seep ourselves, utterly, in the quiet. That's not to say that when we're not traveling that we are not working (We can hear the office support howling with laughter at that one!). In fact we work constantly and must ever play with balancing work/play/stillness on a planet where 2-leggeds have been invited to a quantum leap evolution. Yeeeeehaaaawww! No wonder we get so excited we can't stop sharing the ever growing and adoring words and ways of our Spirits in every way possible. It is our deepest honor and commitment to pass on to you (but only if you are willing) what we have learned from listening to our Spirits day and night. When you read one of our Books, you are reading us a page at a time. Right now you know us better than some of our neighbors!

Thanks for joining us here. That makes our lives worth it. Please stay in touch. Tell us your stories, too. We love that. And let us know how we can support the most amazing journey you can imagine for yourself.

All our love,
Marilyn & Tohmas

www.AhhhMuse.com

Come visit us for more . . .

This is not the end. Here comes the next chapter of a greater, **bigger** adventure where we will meet you again and again! It is the never ending story.

Since we listen to our Spirits every day (gratefully!), life changes, dances, and grows new branches and dreams with every breath. Our Spirits of Creativity—our Muses—always invite us to co-create more miracles with them to integrate the infinite fullness of our beings right here, right now, on this planet Earth: during our workday, in our sleep, while we are brushing our teeth, and most especially, while we are in the shower (Thank you Elemental Water Structuring Shower Units!!!!). In other words, we have tools/ways that integrate the most far-out, far-reaching potentials for the real world, for the 3rd dimension, now.

That is so spectacular, so generous, we must share all of it with you. So, look out! There's going to be some live enthusiasm and love coming your way, because we know that these products/tools/evolutionary gifts work. We use them all. We are the **test bodies** (talk about a fantastic job!!!) for everything that we offer to you now~

"Stones Alive! Vol 1-3"— *The Stonebeings asked us to write new Stones reference books with them. "Yes!" They said they would be new because they would offer their geology and geography, with the profound messages from their hearts. They want to talk and work with us humans to enter this millennium as thriving, loving equals.*

Vibrational Jewelry & Stonessences— *We make these healing tools, ourselves, based upon the Stonecombinations that the Stonebeings offered us, (from the "Stones Alive! Vol 1-3 books) for our most immediate, most supportive and healing evolution, now, e.g.: "Leading with the Heart," "Money Grow," "Connecting with Your Guides," "Bliss," etc.*

Deva's Gift Singing Quartz Bowls and Cosmic Tuner Sets— *The Crystal Deva generously gave us the design for a hand-held Quartz Crystal Singing Bowl. We have faithfully reproduced that design in clear quartz; gold over quartz; platinum over quartz; and gold & platinum over quartz. Plus we are now complementing the bowls with "Cosmic Tuner Sets," which are Stone Wands in the colors of the chakras that can be placed inside the hollow handle of any Deva's Gift bowl to immediately change its vibration to focus on each chakra/issue with which you need spontaneous support. Yes!*

Act of Power Wands— *We make these, ourselves, according to very potent, synergistic combinations that the Stonebeings directly suggested. When you truly choose to heal yourself, these Wands work with you exponentially and compassionately. Besides individual Wands like "Integrating the Mental Body," we very happily offer Wand sets: "Elemental Wands," "Disease into Vitality Wands," and Marilyn's personal favorite, "Planetary Wands."*

Vedic Gemstone Beaded Bracelets— *For millennium, Vedic astrologers have prescribed extremely expensive, flawlessly perfect gemstones to help people work with challenging planets in their astrological birth charts and it has (and still does) offered amazing results in their lives.*

*In listening with the Stones & Crystals, they told us that in this Time of No Time (the transition between the end of the Piscean Age and the beginning of the Aquarian Age), there are different, rapidly-changing Earth energies available that would allow us to utilize less expensive but still potent **combinations** of Stones that through synergy would activate some of that same magnificent astrological support. So we co-created small, beaded Vedic Gemstone Bracelets: exquisite, vibrationally potent, and available at a fraction of the cost of a single Vedic Gemstone. And it gets better . . . we have seven Bracelets, one for every Vedic planet, plus we did an extra overall, grounding combination to integrate all of the planets and all of the energies in your chart at once. Told you it was getting better!*

Elemental Water Structuring Units— *Clean, clear, VITAL food and water, those are our biggest, most joyous priorities. These Units (House, Garden, Shower, or Sink) alchemically, naturally revitalize the water that you drink, cook with, bathe in and absorb and they do it using Stones & Crystals that asked to be in that glorious alchemy!*

Rituals of Manifestation Deck and Guidebook— *The Rituals of Manifestation are 52 cards that present you energies that we all utilize to manifest subconsciously and/or **consciously**. These Deck card messages happily support you to manifest consciously, so that you can actually get the life that you truly wish and are planning, instead of unwanted drama. Yes! And when you need help along the way, the Guidebook generously brings you many words of wisdom from our Spirits and our experiences over lots of years of manifesting miracles consciously. Join us~*

Stones & Crystals— *The Stonebeings call out to us! So we gratefully receive, here, the most potent, the most timely and most unique Stones & Crystals that want to work with humans right now in this overnight quantum leap evolution. We email regular lists of these offerings, letting you know what the Mineral Kingdom is so magnanimously and joyously offering us now. Yes, yes, yes!*

Readings & Workshops— *Our Grandmother has asked us to focus on our services. That is the most immediate way we can offer the wisdom that has been given to us over so many wondrous years. So when you want extra support, ask us for a reading; we are honored to listen to Spirit on your behalf.*

As for workshops, we travel the world, gleefully, sharing every tool and practice that we have at the ready for willing, evolving humans. Our most popular workshop is "Elemental Birth Imprints."

These are just teaser samples of the tools and products and services that we have at the ready to offer you on your unique and perfect journey. So, please, keep connecting with us!!! www.AhhhMuse.com • MQT@AhhhMuse.com 575-534-0410 • 575-654-4757

It is our joy and our honor to meet and know you. This is the most magnificent time on the planet for us to find each other and co-create miracles.

Thank you and blessings always, we offer all our love and support . . .